"Bob's friendship a
us and our marriag
yourself. You'll love ... Bob connects practical insights
with the timeless truth of Scripture. And the suggested activities at the end of each chapter are worth the price of the
book. We enthusiastically recommend this resource."

Robert and Nancy DeMoss Wolgemuth, Authors; founders of Wolgemuth & Associates (Robert) and Revive Our
Hearts (Nancy)

"Bob Lepine's book, *Build a Stronger Marriage*, helps couples
move from unintentionally drifting apart to intentionally
pulling together. Great marriages don't just happen automatically; they are built purposefully. Bob gives readers the
tools to detect marital weak spots and establish new patterns
that bring couples closer together than ever before. A great
resource for any couple who is committed to having, not just
a good marriage, but a great one!"

Sharon Jaynes, Author of *Lovestruck* and *Praying for Your
Husband from Head to Toe*

"I didn't think there was a need for another marriage book,
but then I read Bob Lepine's latest work and was pleasantly
surprised. Bob has concisely and compassionately written a
book that will help marriages at any stage of life. Don't let
the brevity fool you—there is much here for couples to learn
from, savor, and be equipped for."

Jonathan D. Holmes, Executive Director, Fieldstone
Counseling

"Whether you want to repair a broken marriage or make a
healthy marriage stronger, *Build a Stronger Marriage* is the
tool you need. It is also a fantastic resource for counselors
to pass on to the couples they counsel. I plan to keep a few
copies on my shelf to use in my pastoral counseling. The

chapters are short and easy to read but contain truths deep enough to make a lasting impact."

Marty Machowski, Family Pastor; author of *The Ology, Long Story Short, Brave and Bold,* and other gospel-rich resources for church and home

"Here are ten descriptors to say why I think *Build a Stronger Marriage* should be required reading for any couple who wants a lasting marriage: well-written, clear-eyed, grace-saturated, short and potent chapters, winsomely written, pastorally wise, practically applied, refreshingly honest, precise and relevant, and delightfully hopeful."

Dave Harvey, President of Great Commission Collective; author of *When Sinners Say I Do*, *Letting Go*, and *I Still Do*

"Once again, Bob Lepine knocks it out of the park in *Build A Stronger Marriage*. Bob's experience and wise counsel offer specific ways to navigate the common storms of marriage. He asks thought-provoking questions, shares real-life examples to help even the most fragile marriages, and points to the Scriptures for confirmation. Thanks, Bob! Our world needs your insight and encouragement!"

Alex and Stephen Kendrick, Writers, director (Alex) and producer (Stephen), Kendrick Brothers Productions

"For years, Bob Lepine has been teaching us about marriage through our radios, and I am so thankful that now we get the opportunity to learn from his writing. *Build a Stronger Marriage* is a helpful resource from a trusted expert on this most important topic. I plan on giving this book to the mentor couples in our church and using it as our primary marriage ministry resource. I hope your church does the same!"

Dean Inserra, Pastor, City Church, Tallahassee, FL

BUILD A STRONGER MARRIAGE

THE PATH TO ONENESS

Bob Lepine

New
Growth
Press

newgrowthpress.com

New Growth Press, Greensboro, NC 27401
newgrowthpress.com
Copyright © 2022 by Bob Lepine

Unless otherwise indicated, Scripture quotations are taken from the ESV® Bible (The Holy Bible, English Standard Version®). ESV® Text Edition: 2016. Copyright © 2001 by Crossway, a publishing ministry of Good News Publishers. Used by permission. All rights reserved.

Scripture quotations marked as HCSB are taken from Holman Christian Standard Bible, copyright © 1999, 2000, 2002, 2003, 2009 by Holman Bible Publishers, Nashville, Tennessee. All rights reserved.

Scripture quotations marked as MSG are taken from The Message, copyright © 1993, 2002, 2018 by Eugene H. Peterson.

Scripture quotations marked as NIV are taken from Holy Bible, New International Version®, NIV®, copyright © 1973, 1978, 1984, 2011 by Biblica, Inc.® Used by permission. All rights reserved worldwide.

Cover Design: Studio Gearbox, studiogearbox.com
Interior Design and Typesetting: Gretchen Logterman

ISBN: 978-1-64507-307-9 (Print)
ISBN: 978-1-64507-308-6 (eBook)

Library of Congress Cataloging-in-Publication Data on file

Printed in the United States of America

29 28 27 26 25 24 23 22   1 2 3 4 5

To Dennis Rainey,
who recognized long before I did
how central marriage and family are
to the plan of God for humanity.
Thank you for being a coach, mentor, and friend.

CONTENTS

Part 4: Restoring What Has Been Broken

INTRODUCTION

WHY WE'RE HERE:
A REASON FOR HOPE

Let's take a minute to talk about why you're reading this book.

Maybe a pastor or a counselor or a friend suggested you read it. Maybe you picked it up on your own. In either case, you're probably here because something is wrong in your marriage—the relationship you thought would be an ongoing source of joy and love and hope in your life. Now, all that seems far away. Hope has vanished. You're not sure where to find it.

Maybe you and your spouse have drifted slowly toward isolation. You can point to no event that marks where things started to go wrong. It happened gradually. You tell your friends, "We just grew apart."

That slow drift to isolation is a seedbed for resentment. Along the way, husbands and wives look at one another and think, *Why aren't you trying anymore? Why don't you care about me? About us? You promised to love me. What happened?*

The hurt and resentment grow steadily, whether you realize it's happening or not. And one day, you look at each other and think, *There's nothing left here. We're too far gone. I don't see a way back.*

Or maybe you've been on a rough road that led to alienation. You can easily point to the factors that drove the wedge between you. The angry outbursts. The contempt. The criticism. The sarcasm. The emotional abuse.

Maybe specific events led to the division. Financial mistakes. Deep disagreements about how to deal with the kids. Medical issues. An affair. Whatever it was, this is not where you hoped you would be. But you're here. And you're frustrated. Bitter. Resentful.

Maybe you're hanging onto a strand of hope that your relationship can be restored. You've done everything you can think of to try to fix things. But you're hoping maybe someone can point you to something you haven't tried yet, some way to repair the damage and rebuild what is broken.

Or maybe at this point you're thinking you just want all the pain to end. You'll read this book, but honestly, you don't expect anything to change. The patterns in your marriage have hardened. Your heart is cold. You'll read the book because someone said you should or because you want to be able to say you tried everything. But in your mind, your marriage has been over for a long time now, and it's time to move ahead.

That's where my friends Henry and Samantha[1] were early in their marriage. The good-looking, fun-loving college boy Samantha fell for quickly became an angry husband who got angrier when he drank. The night early in their marriage when he became tense and angry during a heated argument left her shaken and ready to get out.

But before she saw a lawyer and filed the paperwork for a divorce, Samantha used her husband's transgressions as justification for her own infidelity. As far as she was concerned, the legal decree was a formality. She was already gone.

Henry and Samantha had both grown up going to church. They had a framework that told them a marriage—even one as badly damaged as theirs was—shouldn't be abandoned without trying to get some help.

Henry took the first step and went to see a counselor. He fully expected that after he outlined his grievances the counselor would see he had no option but to cut things off. He was surprised when the counselor turned the tables on him and forced him to confront his own issues.

And that's exactly what Henry did. He recognized his mistakes and failures as a husband. He saw his issues and began addressing them. He didn't know whether his marriage could be saved, but he was willing to do his part to try.

Samantha started to notice a change in her husband, and she didn't like it. It frustrated her that things that used to trigger his anger weren't setting him off the way they used to. She needed him to continue to be the bad guy in their relationship, so she could more easily justify ending their marriage. Henry wasn't cooperating.

Reluctantly, Samantha went to see the same counselor. Like Henry, she was sure once the counselor heard her side of things he would agree that divorce was the right option. After she laid out her case, she told the counselor that as far as she was concerned the marriage was dead.

She didn't expect his first question. "You said you're a Christian, right? So you believe that God was powerful enough to raise his Son from death to life. But you don't think God can bring your broken marriage back to life?"

That's what this book is all about. We're going to go together on a journey to examine what it will take for your marriage to be restored.

I love the way the Bible talks about God in Isaiah 61. It describes him as a God who comforts those who mourn. A God who can make something beautiful from a pile of ashes. A God who pours out "the oil of gladness" on those who are mourning and gives them a "garment of praise instead of a faint spirit" (Isaiah 61:2–3).

In almost three decades of talking to couples whose marriages were done, I've heard story after story of how God worked in the hearts of the husbands and wives to bring something new and beautiful from the ruins of their relationship. I know it's possible, even in the worst of situations.

Just last night I sat with a couple married almost two decades. They were both at a point where they were ready to reach out for help with the anger issues, the substance abuse issues, the parenting challenges, the health issues, and the financial pressures. The stress in their relationship is real. They were ashamed of the way they had hurt each other. Something has to change, they told me.

We talked for a while. I prayed for them. We discussed the right next steps for both of them. And we made plans to meet again in a few weeks to continue the process of unpacking the accumulated hurts and aches from their years together.

Today, I sent them this text message:

> I wanted to follow up with both of you this morning and let you know how grateful to God I was for your candor, your transparency and your courage in getting together with me last night. I have hope for what God is going to do in your lives and in your marriage and family as you begin to engage and dig a bit deeper into the issues we talked about. In the midst of the stress and discouragement you're facing, know that God is indeed your ever-present help in times of need. He is your rock and your fortress. Cling to Jesus. Hold fast to him. In your weakness, he will become strong. I'm praying for you both today.

I have hope for your marriage too. I don't know your circumstances. But I know the God who brings light into darkness and can raise the dead. He is the One who can repair whatever damage has been done. He can make all things new.

Let me share what I hope this book will do. My goal is to point you to the most common pressure points in marriage.

I fully expect that some of what I address here will not apply to you or your relationship. But I also expect that as you read this, there will be times when you nod your head, highlight a paragraph, and think, *Yep, that's us*. If I can help you see the issues in your marriage more clearly, we're making progress. As Charles Kettering, the one-time head of innovation at General Motors reportedly said, "A problem well defined is a problem half solved."

I also hope you have someone who can walk together with you and your spouse as you read this book. A pastor, a counselor, or a spiritually mature mentor couple will be able to help you apply principles from this book to the specific concerns you are facing in your marriage.

And finally, as you work through this book, I want to urge you to resist the temptation to focus on your spouse's issues or flaws. Jesus warns us against the hypocrisy of addressing the specks we see in our spouse without first looking at the bigger issues present in our own lives (Matthew 7:3–5). The only person you can change is you. So instead of reading this book and hoping it will fix what is wrong with your mate, read it asking God to show you what needs to be addressed in your own life.

Follow the path with me. Let's see together what God is going to do.

PRACTICAL STEPS FOR REAL CHANGE

Each chapter in this book will have a simple assignment for you to complete before you move on to the next chapter. You will be tempted to skip these projects. Don't. This is a vital part of the process that can bring healing to your broken marriage. I'd suggest you write down your answers to these questions in a journal or a notebook.

On paper, write down five issues that have led you to become alienated from each other in your marriage. Be specific. Don't list communication issues and finances. List events or conflicts that have pushed you away from your spouse.

Pray a simple prayer. Look back at the list and say, "God, will you help me see the ways in which I have contributed to the issues that have divided us?" Then write down what comes to mind.

When you're done, look back at the list and pray a second prayer: "God, is there anything I've missed?" Read these verses out loud.

> Search me, O God, and know my heart!
>   Try me and know my thoughts!
> And see if there be any grievous way in me,
>   and lead me in the way everlasting!
>   (Psalm 139:23–24)

Take a minute and be still. Then write down anything else that comes to mind about whatever you've contributed to the issues in your marriage.

You will find yourself wanting to write what seems like a bigger and more important list: all the ways your spouse has damaged your relationship. But that's not the assignment. Focus only on the part you've played.

Pray a final prayer: "God, I confess that I have played a part in our marriage being what it is right now. I confess the things I've done. And I confess the things I should have done that I haven't done. Please forgive me for not being the husband or wife I should have been. Help me, by your Spirit, to be the kind of husband or wife I ought to be. I ask this in Jesus's name. Amen."

PART 1
HOW DID WE
GET HERE?

Chapter 1

MARRIED FOR THE WRONG REASONS

Let's go all the way back to where your relationship began. We'll heed the advice of Fräulein Maria who, while she was still their governess, told the von Trapp children, "Let's start at the very beginning. A very good place to start."

Some of the issues you are facing in your marriage today can be traced back to cracks in the foundation. Specifically, you probably had some pretty superficial motivations at work that led you to the altar. Most of us did.

You also had subconscious expectations about what marriage was going to be like and about how your spouse would act or behave.

And you likely had a shallow and flawed understanding of the real purpose for marriage.

These three foundational issues—motivations for marriage, expectations of marriage, and understanding of the purpose for marriage—can lead to deep disappointments later.

Let's think first about your motivations for getting married. We'll come back to your expectations about marriage and your understanding of the purpose for marriage in upcoming chapters.

Think for a minute about why you walked down whatever aisle you walked down, looked each other in the eye, and at the appropriate time said with a smile, "I do." As best you can determine, what was motivating you to take this life-altering step and pledge your love to one another for a lifetime?

I can tell you what it was for me. It was time.

Mary Ann and I dated for almost four years before I proposed. She was a year ahead of me in college, and when she graduated, she was ready to move into the next phase of life. For her, that meant going to work as a nurse in a local hospital while I finished my senior year. Because we had been a couple all through college, it seemed only right to her that once I graduated the next phase for our relationship would begin as well.

My plan throughout college was to go to law school after graduation. In my mind, the idea of beginning graduate school and starting life as a married couple simultaneously seemed ambitious. For Mary Ann, the idea of continuing to date for some undetermined amount of time wasn't an option. We were either going to move toward marriage, or she was ready to move on.

I knew I loved Mary Ann. I thought she was "the one" (although something in the back of my mind kept asking, *How can you be sure until you've done a little more comparison shopping?*). And two popular songs kept echoing in my head. One was the Beatles song that kept repeating the line "You're gonna lose that girl (yes, yes you're gonna lose that girl)." The other was a song from England Dan and John Ford Coley that declared "It's sad to belong to someone else when the right one comes along."

At the end of the day, the Beatles won. I proposed because I didn't want our relationship to be over. I didn't want to go all the way back to trying to build a new relationship with someone else.

The most common answer couples give to the question "Why did you get married?" is some version of "We were in love." For most, there was some kind of emotional connection that moved them from attraction to bonding, from being interested in each other to making a commitment to one another.

Emotional attraction and bonding may be the most common reason couples become man and wife, but it's far from the only reason.

Maybe one reason you said "I do" was that you were tired of your mom asking you over and over again, "Are you dating anyone yet?"

Maybe you expected marriage to be the cure for loneliness.

Maybe you wanted to have children and raise them in a two-parent family, and you could hear the biological clock ticking.

Maybe you thought, *This person may be my last chance for love*.

Or maybe you thought, as many couples do, that marriage was the right next step. You can't just date or live together in a semi-defined relationship forever. You get to a point where it's time to either get married or break up.

In addition, all kinds of superficial motivations lead people to the altar.

- "He makes me laugh."
- "She comes from money."
- "He's good with kids."
- "She's gorgeous!"
- "We both love [fill in the blank here—food, music, hiking, going to museums, etc.]."
- "He looks great in jeans!"
- "She's really popular."

Any of those dynamics may have been part of what drew you to each other. Attraction and emotional connection aren't wrong. But if you expect those factors to be the glue that holds a marriage together for better or for worse, you're in big trouble.

Stop for a minute. Can you think back to two or three primary motivations that led you to marriage? Before we move on, grab your journal, your notebook, or a plain piece of paper and write down what nudged you toward the altar.

Here's why it can be helpful to revisit our motivations for marriage: *Behind every motivation is a hidden expectation.*

You thought getting married would fix something or solve something or fill in something that was missing. You thought that getting married would mean you'd never be lonely again. Or that you'd always feel safe. Or that your spouse would always desire you or want to be with you. Or that marriage would somehow complete you.

Whatever it was that motivated you to get married quickly became an expectation you had about marriage. We'll look at that next.

PRACTICAL STEPS FOR REAL CHANGE

Look back at your list of the motivations that moved you toward marriage. While in hindsight some of these motivations may have been superficial, they were part of what God used to bring you together as a couple. The bigger issue now is the extent to which these motivations may still be at work in how you view the value of your marriage. Are there still subconscious motivations that are part of how you measure your marriage? Take a few minutes to explore in writing the motivations that continue to affect the way you view your marriage. Then evaluate them.

Chapter 2

NOT WHAT I EXPECTED

Have you ever looked at the one-star reviews for online products? They are often filled with comments from people who expected that the item they were buying would be more dependable, more durable, or more functional than it wound up being. Sometimes the reviews reveal that the buyer had expectations for the product that the manufacturer or seller never promised in the first place.

I'll give you an example. I was shopping recently for a microphone stand. I found one that looked like it would fit my needs, but I decided to check out a few of the one-star reviews first. Here's how one unhappy customer reviewed the mic stand I was considering: "I've never felt so cheated with a purchase. I expected better. When a person purchases a microphone stand with the intention of attaching their mic to it, they shouldn't have to buy a SECOND product that isn't even clearly advertised alongside this. This product should come with a 'microphone holder' PERIOD."[1]

I went back and looked at the product in question. Sure enough, the mic stand is pictured and sold without a mic holder included. The problem this person had with their purchase is not that they didn't get what was promised. It's that they thought the product should deliver *more* than what was promised.

When your marriage turns out to deliver less than what you were expecting, you can easily find yourself writing a one-star review of your spouse in your head!

But hang on. Is it possible that what is out of alignment in your marriage is not your spouse but the expectations you brought with you to the wedding?

I remember asking a couple during premarital counseling about the patterns that had been present in their parents' marriages as they were growing up. "Who took out the trash in your home?" I asked them. "Mom or dad? Who paid the bills? Who cut the grass? Who washed the dishes?" What they discovered as we talked about household responsibilities was, without realizing it, they were heading into marriage expecting their new spouse would do what they had seen their mother or father do.

Mary Ann and I had the same perspective when we married. Throughout the time we dated, Mary Ann had observed a common pattern on Saturday mornings. My practice had always been to sleep as long as possible on this one morning of the week when there was no need to set an alarm. Sometimes this meant I didn't get out of bed on a Saturday until midmorning.

But the first Saturday in our marriage, my new wife was surprised that her husband was still asleep at 9:00 a.m. Mary Ann wakes up early on her own, and on this particular Saturday, she had been awake for three hours already. As the sun had been up for a couple of hours at this point, she decided it was time for her new husband to get up as well. She came into our bedroom and raised the shades.

As I groggily realized that a sleep invader had appeared in my bedroom, I opened one eye and mumbled with astonishment, "What are you doing?"

Later that day, as we talked about our first Saturday morning together as a married couple, Mary Ann told me that her father had always woken up early on Saturday and started into a list of chores or projects. Although that had never been my pattern during our dating years, in the back of her mind was the assumption that, once we were married, I'd become an early riser on Saturdays.

The subconscious expectations we bring with us into marriage touch every part of our relationship. We have hidden expectations about what our relationship will look like, how we will make decisions together, how we'll handle money, how we'll parent—the list is exhaustive! Some of those expectations are reasonable. Many of them are simply our thoughts about the "right" way to do things that we assume our spouse will share. But the idea that two people will think alike about everything is not only unrealistic; it can be unhelpful. We actually need each other to provide a broader perspective on many of the choices we face. As a friend of mine used to say, "If both of you think exactly alike, one of you is unnecessary!"

It's entirely possible that some of the problems you're facing today are a result of the boatload of expectations— realistic and unrealistic—that you carried with you when you walked down the aisle. You believed marriage was created to deliver things it was never designed to produce. You expected your spouse would fulfill needs that a spouse was not designed by God to meet. You expected that your spouse would never disappoint you. And if you're unhappy, somehow you think your spouse must be to blame.

The unrealistic expectations you had for your spouse and your marriage set you up for disappointment from day 1.

Let's pause for a minute again. Think about two or three reasons why you're unhappy in your marriage. Let's examine the expectations behind those areas of disappointment. Here are two fill-in-the-blank questions for you:

- I expected that my marriage would _____

  _____.

- I expected that my spouse would _____
  _____.

This is where you may need some outside help. Some expectations are legitimate. It's not wrong to expect that a spouse will be faithful. Or honest. Or that he or she will not abuse you, physically or emotionally. Not every expectation is unreasonable or unrealistic.

But some are. And talking to a mentor couple, a pastor, or a counselor may help you recognize if your expectations need to be adjusted.

Here's another illustration. Imagine you sent a friend a new washing machine as a wedding gift. Sure it's a lot of money, but he's a good friend. After a month or so, you call your friend and ask, "How's the washing machine working out?" And your friend says, "Well, I hate to say anything because you gave us such a nice gift. But honestly, it's been a catastrophe."

You're stunned. "What's wrong with it?"

"Well, for starters, it completely destroyed my wife's fine china. We loaded the machine up after a big meal, and when the cycle was finished, the plates were in pieces!"

Wait, what?

You ask your friend, "You put dishes in a washing machine?"

"Of course," he says. "Why wouldn't I?"

You may think that anyone should know that a washing machine is for washing clothes, not for cleaning dishes or tools or for giving the dog a bath. But if all you know about a washing machine is that it's for washing things, why wouldn't you toss in dirty pots and pans?

The washing machine clearly isn't the problem here. It's the expectation that's the issue. Apparently, your friend didn't bother reading the manual before using the machine—hence the ensuing disaster and disappointment.

And that brings us to what is maybe the biggest foundation crack in many marriages. Maybe in your marriage.

When you said, "I do," what was your understanding of the central purpose of marriage? Does it match what God had in mind when he said, "It is not good that the man should be alone" (Genesis 2:18)? We'll look more carefully at this idea in the next chapter.

PRACTICAL STEPS FOR REAL CHANGE

We have expectations of one another about all kinds of things, big and small—how we handle money, how we discipline the children, who does what around the house, how often we see our extended families, how often we will be sexually intimate, how tidy the house should be, and how quickly we'll respond to one another's text messages!

What are five specific expectations you have for your spouse? In answering, consider even the subconscious expectations that you carry with you in your marriage every day.

What happens if those expectations aren't met?

How many of your expectations are "deal breakers" for your relationship?

How do you think God would want you to respond when your expectations aren't met?

Remember this: each of you is a flawed, imperfect person. As you disappoint or frustrate one another in marriage, knowing how to give and receive grace is going to be critical. In the same way that you receive grace and mercy from God for your failures and sins, you need to learn how to be regular dispensers of grace to each other.

Chapter 3

THE CENTRAL PURPOSE
OF MARRIAGE

Years ago as I was preparing to speak to a group of engaged couples, I asked a number of pastor friends to share with me the one passage of Scripture they'd want to highlight for soon-to-be-married couples. But there was a catch. I told them they couldn't use any of the "go to" passages from the Bible on marriage. No Ephesians 5:22–33. No Colossians 3:18–19. No 1 Peter 3:1–7. I even took Genesis 2 off the table.

These pastors were quick to offer suggestions. One friend pointed me to Ephesians 4:1–3, where we're called to live with one another in a way that preserves "the unity of the Spirit in the bond of peace." Another pastor friend had me look deeper in that chapter, at the verses that tell us to speak the truth in love (v. 15) and not to let the sun go down on our anger and give the devil an opportunity (vv. 26–27). Still another suggested the end of Ephesians 4, with the instructions on guarding our tongues (v. 29) and forgiving one another (v. 32).

The suggestions kept coming. One pastor brought up the Bible's teaching about spiritual warfare in Ephesians 6. "Remind these couples that, in the midst of conflict, there is an enemy who wants to divide them!" he told me. My list included the first verses of James 4, which talk about reasons for conflict; Colossians 3:5–15, which address putting off old sinful patterns and cultivating new, Christlike habits; and Matthew 7:3–5, which is on Jesus's teaching in the Sermon on the Mount about taking the log out of our own eye before we attempt to remove the speck we see so clearly in our spouse's eye.

Clearly, much in Scripture speaks to how we love one another well in marriage. I'll circle back to some of these passages later in the book.

But I've never forgotten the pastor who said to me, "Pass along the verse I used when I proposed to my wife." And he pointed me to a verse I had read many times before but had never considered as a "marriage" verse: "Oh, magnify the LORD with me, and let us exalt his name together!" (Psalm 34:3).

Have you ever asked yourself about the purpose for your marriage? About why God brought the two of you together as husband and wife? About his intent for making two become one?

The answer is right there in Psalm 34. God joined you as husband and wife so that you could magnify him and exalt his name together.

I have to confess here that magnifying God and exalting his name together with my wife was somewhere way down on my list when Mary Ann and I were married more than forty years ago. I was looking for the joys of companionship. Mary Ann made me feel special and valued, and I liked that feeling. She made me a better person when we were together. And honestly, having someone who would share the household chores and who was interested in sex—those were more front and center in my thinking than any specific ways that our marriage might glorify God.

Companionship and procreation are clearly part of God's purpose for marriage. When the first man was alone in the garden of Eden, God created a suitable companion for him. He created them male and female and told them to be fruitful and multiply.

But his ultimate purpose for bringing the man and woman together was they would become a living representation of the covenant oneness that has bound the three Persons of the Trinity in perfect union and harmony for all eternity. Every husband and wife presents an imperfect picture of that unity in their marriage. God, who knows our weaknesses and frailty, has still chosen that the bond of marriage will be something like performance art, pointing people to the great masterpiece that is the eternal, perfect love that the Father, Son, and Spirit have always enjoyed.

In addition, the Bible tells us that our marriage is designed by God to reflect the loving relationship Jesus has with his bride, the church (Ephesians 5:28–33). Even in the midst of our failures and imperfections, Jesus loves and leads his church, willingly sacrificing himself for us and forgiving us. In response, we trust him, follow him, and submit to him in respect. When our marriage reflects God's design, it models for everyone the glory of God's love for his own.

I know this may all sound abstract. So let me make it practical.

Imagine your marriage is a business. The product you're in business to deliver to your customers every day is a clear picture of the goodness and kindness of God. Your website promises your clientele that they can drop by anytime for a glimpse of the glory of God. Your mission statement for your marriage business is "We exalt God together," just like Psalm 34:3 says.

Now all of a sudden, the question of how the two of you get along as co-owners of the business becomes vitally important. Love and joy and peace and patience and kindness and goodness and faithfulness and gentleness and self-control in your marriage are all key components of a God-glorifying marriage (Galatians 5:22–23). How you relate to and love and serve one another in your marriage is an important part of the product you're in business to deliver.

What am I suggesting here? If your goal is to have a marriage that pleases you, you will face ongoing, perpetual frustration and disappointment. But when your goal is to have a marriage that is pleasing to God, each challenge you face along the way will be a fresh opportunity to fix what's broken and make ongoing progress toward that goal.

Something shifts in your thinking when you move from pursuing joy and happiness in marriage for your own sake and start pursuing it as your ultimate purpose—that God will be glorified in your lives and in your marriage. When both of you can look at one another and say, "What I care about most—even more than my own happiness—is that our marriage is God honoring and God glorifying," you have the right foundation in place for the kind of marriage God brought you together for in the first place.

Having that foundation in place doesn't fix everything. This is only part 1! But getting the foundation right is critical. "Whatever you do," the Bible says, "do all to the glory of God" (1 Corinthians 10:31).

This new way of thinking about marriage will require developing a whole new mindset. Romans 12:2 tells us that the key to transformation is to have our minds renewed. Our default setting in any situation is to ask ourselves what seems right to us. But the Bible tells us to run from that way of thinking! "There is a way that seems right to a man, but its end is the way to death" (Proverbs 14:12). We need to train ourselves to ask whether God has anything to say about this matter. Is there an option here that would be most pleasing to him?

We can't cultivate this new kind of mindset without being people who spend time reading and studying God's Word and who seek God in prayer. These two disciplines are essential if our marriage is going to bring glory to God.

PRACTICAL STEPS FOR REAL CHANGE

Take a few minutes to revisit the motivations for marriage and your expectations for marriage you identified in chapters 1 and 2. Do these motivations and expectations support or detract from having a marriage with God at the center?

Are you ready to move the goal of having a marriage that glorifies God to the center of your relationship? Is your spouse ready? Can you both pray a prayer like this one?

> Father, more than anything, I want your goodness and your kindness to be what people see when they look at our marriage. Help me keep that priority in front of me every day. Help me to make choices with that goal in mind. Help me to give my spouse grace when he/she falls short of that goal. Help me to see my desire for my own happiness as secondary to that higher purpose. Make our marriage about you and not about us. Help us fix what is broken in our lives and in our marriage so that people can see your power and glory on display in us.

Don't think of a prayer like this as a "one and done" moment. This is a prayer you should pray daily to reset your heart and mind on God's purpose for your marriage.

And if you or your spouse can't honestly pray a prayer like this right now, pray that God will help you get to a place where you can sincerely pray it. Can you think of a friend or a mentor—maybe a mentor couple—who could help you in your marriage journey? Send them an email and see if you can get together with them to talk about the work you're doing to strengthen your marriage. Invite them into the process and ask them for their help.

PART 2
WHAT WEIGHS
US DOWN

How we relate to one another in marriage is heavily influenced by past events or relationships that have shaped us. This section of the book is all about helping you explore how significant life events from the past (even past events in your marriage) may be contributing to the challenges you're facing today. Later chapters will help you think about how to address these issues.

Chapter 4

HOW YOUR PAST IMPACTS YOUR PRESENT

Have you ever purchased a used car only to find that the shiny, freshly detailed vehicle that looked great and performed fine on the test drive had a few hidden issues that surfaced after your thirty-day warranty expired?

These days, most used car dealers offer customers a Carfax report for any vehicle on the lot. The report lets dealers and customers know the vehicle history. It includes information about regular maintenance done on the vehicle, accident reports, and data about any major damage done to the car in the past. The Carfax report helps the buyer be aware of what they are getting when they purchase the vehicle.

At this point, no one I'm aware of has come up with a Spousefax service. But when we marry, we bring all of us with us. Our past comes along. We cart along our history of dents and bruises, mistakes and mishaps, trauma and trials. We bring scars. Shame. Self-doubt. And as most couples learn over time, the history each of us brings with us into our new marriage can present us with some unexpected relationship challenges.

Most of what we bring is unseen. In some cases, we aren't even aware of the way our past has shaped who we are.

But as we step into a relationship that is defined by transparency and intimacy, the hidden hurts we bring can surface in unexpected ways. Things that were a part of our growing-up years that we thought were no big deal begin to emerge in our marriage, shaping the way we relate to one another as husband and wife.

Here are some simple examples.

- A wife who was raised by a harsh, authoritarian father can find herself triggered when her gentle and loving husband offers any kind of constructive advice. She imagines he is hiding his true feelings and that he secretly despises her, the way she believes her father hated her.
- A husband who grew up in the shadow of an older sibling who excelled at school or sports can find himself thinking that his wife sees him as second best and wishes she had married someone else.
- A husband or wife who experienced sexual abuse as a child can find it difficult to engage in marital intimacy—without fully understanding why.
- Any childhood experience of loss or trauma can lead to understandable but also unreasonable fears or anxiety as an adult.

If there were such a thing as a Spousefax report, the four areas most important for a prospective spouse to look at are

1. family-of-origin issues,
2. traumas from childhood or young adulthood,
3. issues of shame and guilt related to sex, and
4. unaddressed relational wounds.

Let's take a few minutes with each of those four areas.

PRACTICAL STEPS FOR REAL CHANGE

Someone has said, "Love is blind, but marriage is an eye opener!" Every couple faces surprising revelations that require us to make sometimes challenging adjustments in our lives. Write down two or three things you've learned about your spouse's background that you weren't aware of before you were married.

Have any of these revelations caused you to push your spouse away? Have you resisted making adjustments? Why? If so, ask God to show you better ways you can respond to what you've learned about your spouse since you wed.

Remember, when you begin to uncover issues like these, you may need to ask a mentor, pastor, or counselor to help you process pain from the past and think wisely about how to move forward. Some issues are deep and serious, and getting over them may require outside help.

Chapter 5

YOUR FIRST FAMILY

Early in our marriage, my wife woke up with a pimple on her chin. Being the considerate husband I am, I wanted to make sure she knew it was there. So I said something helpful such as, "Ooh, you have a big pimple on your chin."

Imagine my surprise when my wife looked at me with a shocked expression and asked, "Why would you even say such a thing?" As I remember, she walked away stunned and hurt. I was mystified.

In my family growing up, making a casual observation about a pimple would have been no big deal. But my wife could not fathom why her husband would be commenting on an obvious blemish. She knew she had a pimple. She didn't need me to point it out to her!

For better or worse, all of us first learn how to relate to other human beings in our family of origin. Whatever patterns existed there seemed perfectly normal to us, whether they were actually abusive and harmful or simply ways of interacting based on personality or culture. What we experienced in our family was what we knew. If there was shouting or silence, if we were catered to or ignored, if we laughed a lot or didn't show emotion, even if we were abused and humiliated—whatever we experienced seemed ordinary to us. And what seemed normal helped determine how we would one day relate to others outside our family.

Most counselors and therapists will at some point spend time exploring family-of-origin issues with their clients. They have learned that what happened to each one of us in our childhood years has shaped the person we are today. How we see ourselves and how we relate to others is subconsciously imprinted in our thinking throughout our developmental years. The role of the counselor or therapist is not only to help us see how these patterns developed during our childhood but also to help us understand that what we grew up thinking and believing about ourselves may not be objectively true.

Follow me here. Let's say you had a parent who told you regularly you would never amount to anything. That kind of message from a person in authority, a person you instinctively looked to for love and affirmation and protection and care, burrows deep in your soul. It can be hard later in life to see that for the lie it is. It's hard to unbelieve what you heard repeatedly from a parent.

Years later, that tape keeps playing over and over again in your head, and it impacts the way you relate to your spouse. You think to yourself (at a subconscious level), *The people who were supposed to love me most when I was growing up—my parents—thought I was worthless. I'm guessing this new person who says he loves me—my spouse—probably believes the same thing about me.* The words your parents spoke continue to affect your self-perception and influence your present relationships.

Think about it for a minute. Is it possible that some of the marriage issues you've been experiencing have nothing to do with your spouse? Is it possible you have imported issues that were part of your family of origin into your marriage?

I remember a counselor once telling me that in his years of working with couples, he had concluded that the vast majority of issues in their marriages could be traced back to a failure on the part of one or both spouses to leave father and mother.

Leaving our families of origin to form a new family unit is at the heart of God's design for marriage. In Genesis 2, when

God brings the first man and the first woman together, he establishes this as the normative pattern for marriage: "Therefore a man shall leave his father and his mother and hold fast to his wife, and they shall become one flesh" (Genesis 2:24).

The first step toward a healthy marriage is making a new pledge of allegiance. Leaving our father and mother has more to do with emotional ties than with proximity or geography. Many people whose parents have died are still today bound up in emotional cords, trying to please their parents or gain the approval they never received from them during their lifetime.

Leaving our father and mother means that we begin to see that what our parents said about us, through their words and actions, is not what should ultimately shape our identity. In marriage we become allies with one another, helping each other to embrace and truly believe that what God says about our dignity, value, worth, and significance is truer than the messages we picked up from our parents. The fact that each of us is made in God's image is no insignificant matter (Genesis 1:26). Passages like Psalm 139 that describe us as being "fearfully and wonderfully made" (v. 14) by our Creator speak to the value and dignity of each person. Psalm 8 describes us as being crowned "with glory and honor" (v. 5) by God. One of our assignments in marriage is to become encouragers and cheerleaders, helping our spouse see himself or herself as God sees them.

What you learned about yourself in your family of origin may have shaped the person you have become, but that shaping is not determinative. It can be amended and altered. Your whole sense of self can be reshaped as you decide by faith to believe that what God says is true about you is *really true*. And as you break free from some of those past patterns, you can experience a stronger, healthier marriage relationship—all because you have become a stronger, healthier you.

PRACTICAL STEPS FOR REAL CHANGE

Think about what you grew up believing was true about yourself. Write a list of the top three to five messages you received about your identity from your family of origin.

In what ways has your sense of self affected your relationship with your spouse?

In what ways does your sense of self square with what the Bible says is true about you?

If you are a Christian, the Bible has much to say about who you are in Christ:

- a child of god (John 1:12; Ephesians 1:5)
- loved by god (John 15:13; Romans 5:8)
- a new creation (2 Corinthians 5:17)
- forgiven (1 John 1:9)
- released from shame (Romans 8:1)
- no longer a slave to sin (Romans 6:6–7)
- secure in Christ (Romans 8:35)

The Bible has much more to say about our new identity as followers of Christ. Take a few minutes to think carefully about who you are in Christ. What steps do you need to take to adjust your thinking about yourself to bring it more in line with what God says is true about who you are?

What is one practical way you can encourage your spouse to embrace God's truth about his or her dignity and worth?

Chapter 6

BRINGING TRAUMA INTO A MARRIAGE

My father was twenty-three years old when he and his fellow infantrymen boarded the USS *Susan B. Anthony* on June 6, 1944, headed for Utah Beach on the coast of France. The transport ship he was on hit a mine as it passed through a channel off Normandy. Over the next two hours, the soldiers on board were successfully evacuated and deployed ashore. The sinking of their landing craft was their introduction to a battle that would leave 29,000 of their fellow countrymen dead. For those who survived D-Day, like my young father, the scars remained.

We hear a lot about post-traumatic stress disorder in our day. In an earlier generation, they called it battle fatigue. Men were expected to bottle it up and live with it. Many of those soldiers, like my dad, turned to an actual bottle to help them deal with the trauma they experienced in war.

It's possible that some of the issues you're dealing with in your marriage are tied to traumatic events from your past. Maybe you are an abuse survivor. Maybe you witnessed domestic violence. Maybe one of your parents left. Maybe you were neglected as a child. Maybe your mom and dad divorced. Or maybe a member of your family died. According to the National Child Traumatic Stress Network, "When children have been in situations where they feared for their lives, believed that they would be injured, witnessed violence, or tragically lost a loved one, they may show signs of child traumatic stress."[1]

Any of these things can have effects that last into adulthood and have an impact on your marriage. The experience of profound loss or harm during childhood can leave you vulnerable to fears and anxieties as an adult. When your sense of physical or emotional safety is disturbed, your reflexes adjust. You find yourself flinching or reacting anytime the initial trauma is revisited. You protect yourself by shutting down or by acting out. In addition, because of the prevalence of sexual abuse in our culture, it's common today for couples to experience intimacy issues related to childhood trauma.

If such painful past events are affecting your marriage, simply hoping they will resolve themselves in time will not be enough. You may very likely need the help of someone who can carefully guide you through the process of revisiting, lamenting, and bringing God into the darkness of your trauma.

PRACTICAL STEPS FOR REAL CHANGE

Can you identify any experiences you had prior to marriage that would qualify as traumatic? Anything that left you feeling afraid, unsafe, unprotected, or threatened?

If so, what impact would you (or others) say these events have had on your life and your relationships? Can you see any way the memory of these traumatic events might be creating a wedge in how you and your spouse relate to one another today?

Revisiting trauma from your childhood can be like reopening an old, infected wound. In the same way that you would want a skilled physician to apply his or her expertise to help your body heal from the infection, you may need to invite a trained biblical counselor into the process of revisiting and healing from unaddressed childhood trauma. Your pastor may be able to recommend a skilled counselor who can help you.

In the meantime, you may want to begin processing your thoughts and memories by journaling. Or consider asking a wise, trusted friend to help you go back and revisit some of the painful experiences of your childhood, in order to begin (or continue) the process of healing and moving forward in God's grace.

Chapter 7

CONFRONTING SHAME AND GUILT

There is no easy way to say this, so I'll just get to the point. Odds are you had sex before you were married. Most people getting married today are not virgins. In fact, popular culture has so normalized premarital sex that someone who is waiting until marriage to have sex these days is considered weird or repressed.

You can find plenty of "experts" who will tell you that premarital sex is normal and healthy and good, and that waiting until marriage is somehow a bad idea. In my lifetime, the percentage of people who live together prior to marriage has jumped from 11% to 69%.[1] Additionally, the odds are you've had sex with people other than your spouse. Studies put the average number at somewhere between four and six sex partners prior to marriage.

The point is, if you and your spouse have only ever had sex with each other, and if you and your spouse waited until marriage to have sex, you are maybe not unicorns, but you are certainly part of a small minority of the married population today. If you and your spouse did not bring sexual baggage with you into your marriage, that's no guarantee that your marital sex life won't have issues. Premarital abstinence does not guarantee couples a lifetime of sexual bliss after the wedding. But it can mean you are free from some of the guilt or shame issues other couples experience.

If you are in the majority, however, let's assume for a minute that you had sex with one another or with other people prior to marriage. While that is no longer thought of as a social taboo, it's a clear violation of God's design. Genesis 2:24 talks about two becoming one in marriage. And while there's more to oneness in marriage than sexual union, waiting until marriage to give yourselves to each other sexually is certainly a part of God's plan.

First Corinthians 7 speaks to God's design for sexual monogamy and exclusivity: "each man should have his own wife and each woman her own husband" (v. 2). The Bible lists fornication (sex before marriage) as a sin. And while the culture may scoff, God does not. When we engage in sex outside of marriage, our conscience bears witness that we have sinned against God. We know in our hearts that we've done something we should not have done.

By the way, what the Bible describes as sexual sin goes beyond premarital intercourse. It includes any activities designed to "stir up or awaken" our sexual desire (Song of Solomon 2:7; 3:5; 8:4). Sexual foreplay that stops short of intercourse is not part of God's design for the unmarried. And Jesus says that for a man to look on a woman other than his wife to stir his passions is a manifestation of a sinful heart (Matthew 5:28).

I remember speaking once with a couple who shared openly with me about how their experience of premarital sex affected their marriage. Brad was a freshman in college, and Holly was still a high school senior when found themselves facing an unexpected pregnancy and a hurry-up wedding. Though both of them were Christians, they carried the guilt and shame of their sexual sin with them into marriage. It drove a wedge between them.

The turning point for Holly and Brad came when Holly finally confessed before God that her sexual involvement with Brad prior to marriage had been sinful. In our conversation, Holly said,

> This was not the first time that I told God I was sorry for what I had done. I had told him numerous times that I was sorry for what I had done in the four years previous to this. But . . . I was really sorry that I had gotten caught . . . It's not repentance at all unless you realize and acknowledge to God, "God I have offended you. I have offended your holiness. I had to accept full and total responsibility that this was a sin, it wasn't a mistake, it wasn't an accident, I didn't get carried away. I had full conscious awareness of what I was doing."

Eventually, Holly said, she and Brad repented of their sin together. But she said the initial repentance was personal. "I repented on my own, he repented on his own, and then we came together and asked for forgiveness from each other and asked for forgiveness from God."

Holly went on to tell me that this point of repentance was the beginning of their journey that eventually brought healing in their sex life. It wasn't a quick fix. It wasn't "pray with sincerity and everything will be fine from then on." But confessing their sexual sin was a first step toward a new experience of oneness and the ultimate transformation of their marriage.

Regardless of anything you did before you took your marriage vows, there is hope for you too. Sexual sin can leave scars and have lasting consequences in your life. But God's grace covers all your sins. The great promise of Scripture is, "If we confess our sins, [God] is faithful and just to forgive us our sins and to cleanse us from all unrighteousness" (1 John 1:9). There is freedom from shame and guilt when you repent and believe the gospel. The Bible says, "There is therefore now no condemnation for those who are in Christ Jesus" (Romans 8:1). And I love the way the hymnwriter describes it:

> When Satan tempts me to despair
> And tells me of the guilt within
> Upward I look and see Him there
> Who made an end of all my sin
> Because the sinless Savior died
> My sinful soul is counted free
> For God the Just is satisfied
> To look on Him and pardon me.[2]

It's possible some of the issues you're dealing with in your marriage today have their roots in unresolved shame and guilt from your sexual past. The message of the gospel is that God's grace brings healing and hope.

PRACTICAL STEPS FOR REAL CHANGE

Have you ever confessed to God or to each other your sexual sins prior to marriage? Have you asked for and received forgiveness from each other? If not, you may need the help of a pastor or a counselor in addressing these issues and moving toward freedom from shame and guilt in your marriage.

Chapter 8

THE UNEXPECTED WOUNDS

If you've been married fifteen minutes or longer, you've already sinned against your spouse in some way. You weren't so naive as to think that you'd never hurt each other after the "I dos." You knew that each of you would say or do hurtful things or not say or not do kind things, right?

In marriage, we will be sinned against and will be guilty ourselves of committing a multitude of sins. This is true in all human relationships, but it is especially true in marriage, the closest of relationships. This is why the Bible tells us that "love covers a multitude of sins" (1 Peter 4:8).

Hopefully, both of you are growing in love and grace. Hopefully, you are learning how to live with one another "in an understanding way" (1 Peter 3:7) and are hurting each other less and less. But some hurts go deep. They leave scars. They can leave you walking with a limp in your marriage.

Maybe something your spouse said has lived in your head for years. Or maybe something your spouse didn't say, or has never said, has left you feeling insecure, unappreciated, uncared for, or angry.

You may have been hurt by an action, done carelessly or intentionally, that left you feeling unloved. Or you may have resigned yourself to the reality that your spouse isn't going to do certain things that you've always wished he or she would do. These omissions, intentional or not, can also leave scars on your soul.

The old adage that time heals all wounds isn't true. Yes, the pain you experience when your spouse says something hurtful will likely fade over time. But some of those hurtful words become lodged in your heart. They come quickly to mind when things become stressful in your relationship.

Anytime I've met with a couple who is looking for help, I hear about words or actions, sometimes from years ago, that have crippled their relationship. Most often, it's not a single act or an isolated statement that continues to plague the marriage but an ongoing pattern of actions or words that produce fresh wounds over and over again. But there are times when a single particularly hurtful incident or a harsh comment does profound damage.

You want to know what is the most common, and probably the most hurtful, statement couples make to one another? It's when, in the middle of conflict, a husband or wife looks at the other person and says, "Maybe we never should have gotten married in the first place!" Or the even more deadly statement, "Maybe we should get a divorce."

Have you said something like that to your spouse? Or have you heard a threat like this from your spouse? If you have, a poison was released that threatens the core of your relationship. In an instant, with a reckless statement, you or your spouse sowed a seed that leaves one or both of you wondering if the commitment you made to one another is secure. Either of you can find yourself feeling insecure and thinking, *One wrong word or wrong action, and my spouse might be gone*. All of a sudden, the safety and security that a marriage covenant is supposed to provide is gone. "Till death do us part" is no longer something you can count on.

In the next chapter, we'll think together about the biblical principles we can follow to bring healing and forgiveness to a wounded relationship. Cleaning out the marital bed of weeds and uprooting the bramble choking the life out of your marriage can take time. Revisiting the hurt can be painful.

But at the risk of mixing metaphors, if your marriage is going to heal, some broken bones may need to be reset, or some infected wounds may need to be sterilized.

The elements I've identified in this part of the book—family of origin issues, childhood or young adult trauma, guilt and shame issues, or marital wounds—any or all of these can weigh a relationship down. They all move marriage partners toward isolation. We drift apart instead of coming together.

Don't be discouraged if a lot has been unearthed in these past few chapters. Recognizing the issues present in our marriage is a first step toward fixing what's broken. Yes, it can feel overwhelming. But God's promise is that as we walk this journey with him, he will replace the ashes of our marriage with a crown of beauty. Instead of a spirit of heaviness, he says, he'll give us "the oil of gladness." He will replace our weakened spirit with a "garment of praise." He will rebuild the ancient ruins (Isaiah 61:3–4).

PRACTICAL STEPS FOR REAL CHANGE

Are there things you have said or done to your spouse that has hurt them?

Are there words or actions from your spouse that easily come to mind that continue to be source of hurt or pain for you? Can you list them (no more than five)?

Are there things you wish your spouse would say or do that have been absent from your marriage?

Chapter 9

TIME TO FORGET
A FEW THINGS

We all have a past. And to some extent, the events of your past have marked and molded you into the person you have become today. Your past does not determine your future. But the events that have shaped your life to this point—the successes and the scars, the triumphs and the trauma, the glory and the guilt—all of it mixes together in your soul and spills out in a variety of ways, including the way you relate to your spouse.

What do you do with family-of-origin issues that still impact how you think and choices you make today? What's a workable strategy for processing childhood or young adult trauma? Is there a way to drain shame and guilt of its power over you? And what do you do with the hurt you've experienced from the person who promised to love, honor, and cherish you?[1]

The wounds and pain and trauma of the past are powerful. They can be *strongholds* in your life. In the Bible a spiritual stronghold is any experience, thought, idea, or philosophy that keeps you from living life as God intends, walking in freedom, joy, and hope. The enemy of your marriage—the devil—is skilled at using events and memories from your past to disrupt God's good purposes for your marriage.

The Bible tells us to tear down these strongholds. We do this by taking our thoughts captive: "For though we walk in the flesh, we are not waging war according to the flesh. For the weapons of our warfare are not of the flesh but have divine power to destroy strongholds. We destroy arguments and every lofty opinion raised against the knowledge of God, and take every thought captive to obey Christ" (2 Corinthians 10:3–5).

The apostle Paul, who wrote those words, knew something about how events from the past have to be confronted. In writing to the Philippians, Paul dug into his own past history, a history filled with pride and a toxic sense of spiritual superiority. Paul's self-righteous zeal turned him into a passionate persecutor of Christians in the early years of the church. He cheered on his fellow Pharisees as they hurled rocks at the first Christian in history to be martyred for his faith.

That past hatred of Jesus and the early church came back to haunt Paul after Jesus appeared to him on the road to Damascus, asking him, "Why do you persecute me?" The guilt and shame he felt as one who was complicit in the persecution and murder of Christians were real and present and powerful. It had to be addressed.

Paul knew he couldn't change his past. You can't change your past either. But he also knew he had access to a divine power that could destroy the stronghold of his past. He knew some things had to be wrestled with, confronted, and ultimately forgotten. As he wrote to the Philippians, "one thing I do: forgetting what lies behind and straining forward to what lies ahead, I press on toward the goal for the prize of the upward call of God in Christ Jesus" (Philippians 3:13–14).

What did Paul mean when he spoke of forgetting what was behind? Clearly he hadn't forgotten his past. He had just summarized the high points in his letter. But Paul knew he had to bring the truth of the gospel to bear on his past sins and hurts. He had come to believe that what Jesus said about his new identity in Christ was more real, more powerful, and truer than the strongholds that controlled him. He confronted his past, asking God to bring healing and to take away the guilt and shame. That's ultimately what enabled him to take his own thoughts about his past captive.

Essentially, what Paul did is what each of us has to do: believe that the truth of the gospel is more powerful than the truth of our past—believe that God's power to heal, forgive, and redeem the past is stronger than Satan's power to condemn, accuse, and hold us hostage.

The Bible tells us that the omniscient God—the God who knows all and sees all—has chosen, for all who have surrendered their lives to Jesus, to "remember their sins no more" (Hebrews 8:12). That doesn't mean God can't recall the events of your life. It means he has put your sins out of sight. Because of what Jesus did, paying the penalty for your sin, God put those sins "as far as the east is from the west" (Psalm 103:12), "into the depths of the sea" (Micah 7:19), and behind his back (Isaiah 38:17). God purposely, actively, and deliberately puts your sins out of his mind. If you are in Christ, when God sees the sins of your past, he sees the blood of Christ covering them.

As for the hurts and wounds of your past, God invites you into his great restoration process. He says, "Bring me your ashes, and together we can make something beautiful from them."

I'm not suggesting that the sins of your past—the ones you committed or the ones committed against you—can be easily and quickly wiped away. Some wounds go deep. Some scars take a long time to heal. And it's possible you will need a pastor or a counselor to help you work your way through the process.

But here's what's at stake. Your marriage. Your family. Your future. With many couples—maybe with you—what feels like a marriage issue is really a wound or scar from the past that is showing up today in your most important relationship. You may see your spouse as the issue. But what if the issue is not your spouse but your scars?

One final thought before we move on: if you find yourself thinking, *My marriage issues don't have anything to do with childhood trauma or family-of-origin issues or past guilt and shame*, then before you rush past all that we've talked about here, take some time with God, asking him to confirm your conclusion. Ask him whether unresolved issues from your past might be leaking toxic fumes into your marriage today. Don't discount the impact your past may have on your life and your relationships today.

PRACTICAL STEPS FOR REAL CHANGE

I want you to read through some song lyrics, written by singer/songwriter Bob Bennett, who had to get help working through how his past was sabotaging his life and his relationships as an adult. Here is what he wrote:

> Every harsh word spoken
> Every promise ever broken to me
> Total recall of data in the memory
> Every tear that has washed my face
> Every moment of disgrace that I have known
> Every time I've ever felt alone
>
> All the chances I let slip by
> All the dreams that I let die in vain
> Afraid of failure and afraid of pain
> Every tear that has washed my face
> Every moment of disgrace that I have known
> Every time I've ever felt alone
>
> Lord of the here and now
> Lord of the come what may
> I want to believe somehow

That you can heal these wounds of yesterday
So now I'm asking you
To do what you want to do
Be the Lord of the past
Oh how I want you to be the Lord of the past.[2]

Read the lyrics again, slowly. This time, when you read "every harsh word spoken," ask God to bring to mind harsh words spoken to you in the past that may still be a source of pain in your heart today. Do the same thing with every line in the two verses of the song.

Then when you get to the chorus, make it a prayer. Ask God to be the Lord of your past. Ask him to make something beautiful from your ashes.

And memorize 1 John 1:9: "If we confess our sins, he is faithful and just to forgive us our sins and to cleanse us from all unrighteousness." Recite this verse out loud every morning and every evening. Make it an ongoing practice to regularly confess to God any known sins. As you do, say, "Thank you, God, for forgiving my sins and for cleansing me."

PART 3
THE ESSENTIAL OIL
IN EVERY HEALTHY
MARRIAGE

Chapter 10

ARGH! SOMETIMES MY SPOUSE MAKES ME SO ANGRY!

You know how people always say there are only two certainties in life—death and taxes? I'll add a third: marital conflict. It's inevitable. If someone says to you, "We don't have any conflict in our marriage," check their pulse. Conflict happens. We offend each other.

The Bible talks about conflict in relationships. James asks the question "What causes quarrels and what causes fights among you?" (4:1). He doesn't ask, "Do you have quarrels and fights?" He presumes you do. We all do. He wants you to look under the surface at why you quarrel and fight.

He then gives the answer. He says your quarreling and fighting are rooted in the fact that when things don't go the way you think they should, or the way you want them to, you get angry. You look around for someone to blame. You determine that someone else is the reason you're angry instead of stopping to consider whether your desires and passions were true or right or good in the first place.

In marriage, we often are provoked to anger when our spouse doesn't meet our expectations, whether that involves keeping a clean house, being on time, or how often we make love. Quarreling and fighting are usually provoked when we fall short of each other's expectations.

I remember hearing a friend offer an insightful observation years ago. In response to a wife who said, "I was never an angry person until I got married," my friend said, "You were always an angry person. It just took the right person to expose what has been inside you all along!"

Nobody can make you angry. Someone else is not responsible for your anger. You are.

I'm not suggesting that your spouse bears no blame for the discord that may exist in your marriage. Your spouse is almost certainly guilty of acting in ways that are selfish, uncaring, and unloving. He or she may be doing things that are cruel and evil. There are likely issues in your spouse's life that need to be addressed and confronted. We'll get to that, trust me.

But here, let's focus on your anger.

First, we should acknowledge that not all anger is sinful. There is such a thing as righteous anger. God gets angry at sin and injustice. His anger is holy. It's not tainted with any hint of sin. In fact, his perfect anger is perfectly counterbalanced by his tenderhearted compassion and his lovingkindness toward us.

I'm guessing that most of the time when you're angry, tender compassion and lovingkindness are nowhere to be found. So while there is such a thing as righteous anger, let's face the fact that most of the time your anger doesn't fit that definition. Most often, your anger isn't righteous anger. It's self-righteous anger.

Anger is sometimes referred to as a secondary emotion. That is to say, before you become angry, something else you're feeling ignites the anger. The most common emotions that lead to anger are hurt or fear—or both. When your safety or security is threatened, when you feel vulnerable or at risk, your defense mechanisms kick in. You shift into protection mode. You lash out at the person you see as a threat in a subconscious attempt to get that person to back down. Many times what you're saying, when you manifest anger toward another person, is, "You're scaring me" or "You're hurting me. Stop it!"

The truth is, getting angry almost never makes anything better. It won't fix your marriage or resolve any conflict. That's not what anger does. Anger tears down and destroys. It doesn't build up. The Bible puts it this way: "the anger of man does not produce the righteousness of God" (James 1:20).

If your goal is to bring healing and restoration to your relationship, you must do something about your anger. You're going to have to learn how to put it away. That's what we're told to do in Colossians 3: "Put to death therefore what is earthly in you . . . put them all away: anger, wrath, malice, slander, and obscene talk from your mouth" (vv. 5, 8).

How do you put sinful anger to death? First, you see it for what it really is—sinful anger. You quit justifying it. You don't minimize it. You call it what it is. It's not frustration or irritation or being annoyed. It's self-centered, self-righteous anger.

Next, you quit coming up with excuses. You quit blaming the other person. You go to God and confess that your anger is a sin against him and against your spouse. You own it instead of having it own you.

Third, you train yourself to respond differently to the anger impulse. When your stomach tightens and your face starts to flush and you're ready to boil, you remind yourself that Jesus said, "Love your enemies, do good to those who hate you, bless those who curse you, pray for those who abuse you" (Luke 6:27–28). Instead of moving to anger, move to prayer. Instead of lashing out, choose to do good. Instead of cursing, bless.

Remind yourself of what 1 Peter 3:9–12 says:

Do not repay evil for evil or reviling for reviling, but on the contrary, bless, for to this you were called, that you may obtain a blessing. For

"Whoever desires to love life
   and see good days,
let him keep his tongue from evil
   and his lips from speaking deceit;
let him turn away from evil and do good;
   let him seek peace and pursue it.
For the eyes of the Lord are on the righteous,
   and his ears are open to their prayer.
But the face of the Lord is against those who do evil."

Finally, it's not enough to work to put anger to death. We have to work to replace anger with godly character. In the same passage in Colossians 3 where we're told to put anger to death, we're told to "put on then, as God's chosen ones, holy and beloved, *compassionate hearts, kindness, humility, meekness, and patience*, bearing with one another and, if one has a complaint against another, forgiving each other; as the Lord has forgiven you, so you also must forgive. And above all these put on love, which binds everything together in perfect harmony. And let the peace of Christ rule in your hearts, to which indeed you were called in one body. And be thankful" (vv. 12–15, emphasis added).

That's a tall order, right? But it's what God is calling you to in your marriage. Not to anger and malice and slander and abusive speech. But to "love, joy, peace, patience, kindness, goodness, faithfulness, gentleness, self-control" (Galatians 5:22–23). There's a reason the Bible calls these godly character qualities "the fruit of the Spirit." On your own, you will regularly slip back into destructive patterns and habits in your relationship. But as you walk by the Spirit, he is the one who produces this kind of godly fruit in your life.

Anger is a losing strategy for oneness in marriage. Anger pushes us apart. It doesn't pull us together. And anger breeds anger. It escalates conflict. It doesn't solve anything. Put it to death.

PRACTICAL STEPS FOR REAL CHANGE

Think about the most recent time you were angry at your spouse (or frustrated with or annoyed at them). What were you afraid of in that moment? Or what were you hurt by? Or what did you want that you didn't get? What aspects of your anger were legitimate or justified? What aspects were self-centered or self-righteous? Write out your answers. Ask God to show you what part of your anger was sinful. And then confess your sins to him. And to your spouse.

God's call to replace anger with compassion and kindness and blessing is counterintuitive. It can sound risky or wrongheaded. Can you embrace the goodness of God's design here? Can you, by faith and in reliance on him, do what he is calling you to do?

Chapter 11

OVERLOOK? OR CONFRONT?

Every time you experience conflict in marriage, you find yourself at a crossroads. You've been hurt. Offended. Sinned against. The peace you long for in your marriage has been broken. What do you do?

There are two choices here. Overlook it. Or confront it.

Let's talk about what overlooking an offense looks like. This is important. Because it should be the option you choose most often. You want to get this right.

First, overlooking an offense is commended in the Bible. "Good sense makes one slow to anger," the book of Proverbs tells us, "and it is his glory to overlook an offense" (19:11). Again, "Hatred stirs up strife, but love covers all offenses" (Proverbs 10:12). The New Testament makes the same point. "Above all," Peter writes, "keep loving one another earnestly, since love covers a multitude of sins" (1 Peter 4:8).

Let's be clear though. Choosing to overlook an offense doesn't mean you internalize it. Or stuff it. Overlooking an offense involves more than deciding not to say anything about it. It means you make a choice to pour grace all over someone's transgression. It means you make a choice not to hold the offense against your offender.

Why would you overlook an offense? For a lot of reasons. First, because you realize that this specific offense really isn't that big a deal. Your spouse promised to stop at the store on the way home, and he forgot. Or she was cleaning out a closet and threw away by mistake a souvenir program from a sporting event you went to seven years ago. At the end of the day, you realize that in those kinds of situations, what your spouse is really guilty of is being human. You make the choice to let it go.

You decide to overlook an offense because you realize that you're human too. You've messed up. Overlooking an offense is a humble, gracious choice. And you overlook because no one has the time or energy to confront every minor transgression.

So why would you decide not to overlook an offense? For two reasons.

First, because you've tried to let it go, but you just can't. The memory of the offense keeps coming up. The emotions remain fresh. You can tell a root of bitterness is growing in your soul, and to help you move on, you need your offender to hear clearly how the offense hurt you.

Or you may choose to confront an offender because the offense represents a recurring pattern in your spouse's life that he or she either isn't aware of or doesn't realize is a big issue. Here, the decision to lovingly and gently confront your spouse is motivated by your desire to help your spouse grow in godliness and not by your inability to let go of the offense.

Galatians 6 lays out the pattern for this kind of confrontation: "Brothers, if anyone is caught in any transgression, you who are spiritual should restore him in a spirit of gentleness" (v. 1a). There's a lot to think about there.

- Is your spouse stuck in some kind of ongoing sin pattern?
- Do you have the spiritual clarity and discernment about this issue that you'll need to be able to have the conversation with your spouse?
- Have you prayed about whether God would have you confront him or her?
- Is your goal to see your spouse walking in freedom and victory?

- And can you maintain a spirit of gentleness while you confront him or her?

There's more. "Keep watch on yourself," the Bible says, "lest you too be tempted" (v. 1b). When we step in to help free someone who is caught in a pattern of sin in his or her life, we are stepping onto a spiritual war zone. We are engaging with a spiritual enemy who wants to keep our spouse ensnared and who will oppose our efforts. Seeking to help someone who is in spiritual bondage is not a casual endeavor. We should be ready for battle.

But our assignment is clear. "Bear one another's burdens, and so fulfill the law of Christ" (v. 2). We are called by God to engage and to help others get free from spiritual bondage in their life.

The decision to confront an offense is not something anyone should do casually or carelessly. If it's not a Spirit-led decision, it will likely do more harm than good.

PRACTICAL STEPS FOR REAL CHANGE

First, pray. Ask God to reveal any ways in which your spouse has wounded you that are still lodged in your heart. Make a list of specific instances where your spouse has offended or hurt you.

Now, look at your list, and pray again. Ask God for wisdom about offenses you should choose to overlook. Make the decision to let go of any lingering bitterness or resentment or hurt arising from those particular offenses. Choose to pour grace over them, realizing that God has poured his grace over your sins against him.

If there are items on your list that you believe require confrontation, read back through Galatians 6:1–2 and ask God to make your heart right before you move forward. And once you think you're ready, take one final step: read chapter 12 of this book first.

Chapter 12

WITHOUT THIS, YOUR MARRIAGE WON'T MAKE IT

Here's a primer on the internal combustion engine. It's the kind of engine most of us have in our cars. It's what moves the car from place to place. The mixture of fuel and fire in the engine create a lot of heat and a lot of friction. That's why your engine is continually bathed with oil. It keeps the friction from destroying the engine and bringing the car to a grinding halt.

Every marriage has elements that produce heat and friction. And unless your marriage is continually bathed with the oil of grace and the ability to forgive one another, you can expect your marriage to seize up, just like an engine that has no oil in the crankcase.

Ruth Bell Graham, the wife of noted evangelist Billy Graham, said once that a happy marriage is the union of two great forgivers.[1] She's right. There can be no oneness in marriage unless we learn how to forgive and ask for forgiveness.

For followers of Christ, forgiving others is nonnegotiable. It's not optional. The prayer Jesus taught his disciples assumes they are practicing forgiveness: "forgive us our debts, as we also have forgiven our debtors" (Matthew 6:12). He went on to make it clear that it is characteristic for someone who has been forgiven by God to forgive others (Matthew 6:14–15).

And he's not talking about a one-time act. When the disciples ask him how often they should forgive someone who has offended them, they pose the question this way: "Lord, how often will my brother sin against me, and I forgive him? As many as seven times?" Because the Jews saw the number seven as signifying completeness, the question was really "do I keep on completely forgiving someone who sins against me?" Jesus's response drives home the point about the significance of being ready to forgive another person. "I do not say to you seven times," Jesus said, "but seventy-seven times" (Matthew 18:21–22).

Don't just forgive completely. Forgive completely, then do it again. And again. And again.

Do you find yourself hesitant to extend forgiveness? I get that. You may be thinking that granting forgiveness means that your spouse is now free to repeat the same behavior. You're thinking you've given him or her a get-out-of-jail-free card. Unless there is some kind of punishment that stings, you reason, your spouse will think, *I got away with it that time*, and will be likely to repeat the offense.

So what do we do with Jesus's words about forgiving over and over again? Ignore them? Withhold forgiveness until we're convinced our spouse is really, really sorry?

I propose that the solution here is for us to think a little more carefully about the whole subject of forgiveness. We need to look closely at what the Bible says about the right way to seek forgiveness when we have sinned against our spouse and about the right way for us to extend forgiveness when we've been sinned against.

The Bible has a lot to say about forgiveness—more than we can look at here. But when we add it all up, we find that forgiveness is a core theme in Scripture. The message of the gospel is that God has graciously chosen to forgive stubborn, stiff-necked, rebellious men and women like you and me.

We are never more like Jesus than when we choose to forgive someone who has wronged us.

We'll discuss forgiving our spouse in the next chapter. But for now, let's talk about the right way to seek forgiveness when we've messed up.

Seeking forgiveness is a two-step process that centers on confession.

Confession occurs privately first. Before you confess to the person you've offended or wronged, you confess to yourself and to God. You own the weight of what you've done. And you agree with God that your actions or attitudes have been wrong and are an offense to him.

Confession doesn't end once you've gone to God. You have to go to your spouse to seek his or her forgiveness. You take responsibility for your actions. You don't shift the blame to someone else. You don't make excuses. You don't minimize your mistakes. Confession sounds like this: "I did it; it was wrong. I'm to blame, and I'm sorry. Will you forgive me?"

You make sure you've not just cobbled together the right words so you can get back in your spouse's good graces. A half-baked confession is no confession at all. Saying something you don't really mean or don't really believe is true just to get your spouse off your back is manipulative and dishonest. It's like duct tape. It may patch things up temporarily, but it's not a fix. It doesn't bring oneness.

Ultimately, confession involves asking your spouse to give you what you acknowledge you don't deserve: grace and forgiveness.

In the 2008 movie *Fireproof*, the lead character, Caleb, begins to see how he has sinned against his wife, Catherine. He has no idea whether his marriage can be salvaged. But he reaches a point where he realizes that he needs to ask her forgiveness for how he has wounded her. Here's what he says: "Catherine . . . I need you to understand something. I am sorry. I have been so selfish. For the past seven years, I have trampled on you with my words and with my actions. I have loved other things when I should have loved you. In the last few weeks God has given me a love for you that I had never had before. And I have asked him to forgive me. And I am hoping, I am praying that somehow you would be able to forgive me too."[2]

What's significant about that confession is what's not in it. There is no blame shifting. No excusing the sin. No "I'm sorry if . . ." or "I'm sorry, but . . ." Caleb doesn't bring up how Catherine has sinned against him. It's a straightforward, clear, clean owning up to what he's done wrong and a humble request for grace.

That kind of confession is essential. But if you're really going to seek another person's forgiveness, you need to do more than admit your failings; you need to make it clear that going forward your intent is to change—to not repeat the sinful patterns. In a word, you need to not just confess but to repent.

Repentance means turning around and heading in a different direction. Whereas confession is admitting that what you did in the past was wrong, repentance is declaring your intention to make different choices going forward. When you confess, you're saying, "I'm sorry. I was wrong. Will you forgive me?" When you repent, you're saying, "I will make it my aim to not do again what I did that was hurtful or harsh. I will do all I can to make a different choice next time."

When you become aware that you have wronged your spouse, you have a responsibility to confess and repent—to "seek peace and pursue it" (Psalm 34:14).

PRACTICAL STEPS FOR REAL CHANGE

Are you aware of specific ways you have sinned against your spouse? Things you've said? Done? If someone asked your spouse for a list of ways you've hurt him or her, what would be on that list? And before you dismiss any of it with a "she's overreacting" or "it was his fault too," ask God to help you see clearly the things that you need to own, regardless of any other factors at play.

Make a list of the specific sins. Confess them to God as sins not only against your spouse but against him as well. Read Psalm 51, where David prays a prayer of confession after having committed adultery. Notice how he prays to God, "Against you, you only, have I sinned and done what is evil in your sight" (v. 4).

Now find a time when you can get with your spouse and confess to him or her. If you're going to be confessing sins that your spouse is currently unaware of, realize that you are going to be opening a wound that may take time to heal. Seek counsel ahead of time. Pray. Make sure your heart is humble, broken, and contrite. Don't become defensive or make excuses. Own your sin. And ask your spouse to forgive you.

Chapter 13

WHAT FORGIVENESS IS (AND WHAT IT ISN'T)

Love, according to 1 Corinthians 13, does not allow resentment to take up residence in a relationship. In some Bible versions, here's how 1 Corinthians 13:5 is translated: Love "does not keep a record of wrongs" (HCSB). Love wipes the books clean. Debts are canceled. The debtor is forgiven, and no payment is required.

I've met plenty of people who have been so wounded by a spouse's sin against them that, for them, forgiveness is out of the question. I've heard spouses say things like, "I've forgiven her, but I'll never speak to her again!" indicating a deficient understanding of what forgiveness means. Imagine God saying the same thing about us!

So let's talk about what forgiveness is and what it isn't. To do this, I'm going to discuss two types of forgiveness: personal forgiveness and relational forgiveness. Personal forgiveness is a choice you make on your own to let go of your right, real or perceived, to punish another person for how they have harmed you. Relational forgiveness is a transaction that takes place when two people follow a biblical pattern for pursuing peace and reconciliation in their relationship.

Let's consider personal forgiveness first.

There's an expression we use when we think about making peace with someone else; we talk about "burying the hatchet."

I've often joked with couples about that expression. What were you doing with a hatchet in your hands in the first place? You were on the warpath! You were looking for a chance to do harm to someone who had attacked or injured you.

Burying the hatchet is a way of saying that you are putting away the right or desire to demand payback for how you've been wronged. Forgiveness is the opposite of "an eye for an eye and a tooth for a tooth" (Matthew 5:38–42).

In contrast, unforgiveness holds on to the demand that the debt against you be settled with an equal or greater infliction of pain. With unforgiveness, you are not satisfied that the debt is settled until the person who hurt you has also been hurt, with a level of pain that will serve as a deterrent to any future injury against you. In this scenario, you see your spouse as a criminal who has to pay his debt to society (or to you) with enough jail time and hard labor to ensure he or she has been rehabilitated and will not harm you again. The emphasis here is on wanting justice to be done.

But here's the thing about pursuing justice: we think in the back of our minds that seeing someone pay for their crimes will help ease the pain we feel from the injury we've suffered. But it doesn't work that way. Someone else experiencing pain doesn't diminish our pain. Demanding justice and failing to forgive does not bring peace or joy to our soul.

What I'm calling personal forgiveness, then, is the choice you make to release your spouse from the debt they owe you for the harm they've done. It's a decision not to keep a record of their wrong. You drop the charges. You hand the matter over to God, the righteous Judge, and let him sort things out as he chooses (Romans 12:19).

Choosing to forgive your spouse doesn't mean the hurt goes away. You may still feel lingering pain for the hurt you've experienced or the harm that has been done to you even after you have given up the right to punish them.

Some people think that forgiving someone means you have to be able to forget the wrong that was done. But that's not the case. Think about marital infidelity. Do you think that anyone whose spouse cheated on them ever comes to a point in their marriage where they forget the infidelity ever happened? The memory and the pain of betrayal will fade over time, but that's something no one ever forgets. Scars remain.

Still, a betrayed spouse can make a decision to say, "I forgive you for what you've done to me." Ken Sande, in his book *The Peacemaker*, outlines the four promises we are making when we choose to forgive our spouse.

1. "I will not dwell on this incident."
2. "I will not bring up this incident again and use it against you."
3. "I will not talk to others about this incident."
4. "I will not let this incident stand between us or hinder our personal relationship."

"By making and keeping these promises of biblical forgiveness," Sande says, "you can tear down the walls that stand between you and your offender. You promise not to dwell on or brood over the problem or to punish by holding the person at a distance. You clear the way for your relationship to develop unhindered by memories of past wrongs. This is exactly what God does for us, and it is what he calls us to do for others."[1]

Those four promises do not require anything on the part of the offender. They are all choices you make when you choose to forgive. That's why this first level of forgiveness is personal. It's a decision on your part to live out the mandate found in Romans 12:18: "If possible, so far as it depends on you, live peaceably with all."

And personal forgiveness can be granted regardless of whether your spouse ever confesses his or her sin, seeks forgiveness, or repents. You can decide to bury the hatchet on your own.

Relational forgiveness is another layer. While personal forgiveness is a necessary first step in the direction of pursuing peace with your spouse, it doesn't restore what's been broken relationally. That involves a next step. For a relationship to be truly mended, two people have to take steps together that can lead to reconciliation and restoration.

Sometimes personal forgiveness is all you can do. It may be that the person who harmed you has died. Or they might be unrepentant, refusing to acknowledge their sin against you or the harm they've done to you. In such a situation, the decision to release the one who hurt you from punishment is a choice you make on your own, in response to God's call for you to forgive those who have trespassed against you (Matthew 6:12).

But when your spouse comes to you confessing, repenting, and seeking your forgiveness, as we talked about in the previous chapter, you have to be ready to start moving in the direction of granting the relational forgiveness your spouse is seeking. Jesus is clear on this. "If your brother sins," he says, "rebuke him, and if he repents, forgive him, and if he sins against you seven times in the day, and turns to you seven times, saying, 'I repent,' you must forgive him" (Luke 17:3–4). Children of God are forgiven people. And forgiven people forgive people. It's what we do.

Like personal forgiveness, relational forgiveness means that you apply the four promises outlined earlier. You put the matter to rest, once and for all. You never bring it up again. You don't hold it over your spouse's head. When the thought of their sin against you comes to mind, you take that thought captive and put it away. You don't talk about it with others. And you don't allow it to be a wedge that keeps you isolated from your spouse.

What do you do if your spouse comes to you seeking forgiveness, and you're just not ready? It's okay to say, "I need time." What's not okay is for that time period to stretch on for weeks.

Forgiveness is an act of grace. When you find yourself unable to forgive, your assignment is to go to God and ask him for the grace you need. When you can't forgive your spouse, God can forgive him or her *through you*. Ask him to pour his love and grace into your life and heart and to make you a channel of that love and grace to your spouse. Take the step of faith God is calling you to take. Give your spouse what God has given so freely to you. Extend generous forgiveness.

Here's an important caveat. Forgiveness is a step in the direction of reconciliation. But it's only the first step. For a relationship to be rebuilt, trust has to be reestablished.

Imagine your teenage son arrives home one evening with bad news. He was driving too fast, wasn't paying attention, got in a wreck—and now the car is totaled. He is clearly sorry for what he's done and is willing to own his mistake. He expresses his intent to slow down and pay more careful attention to what he's doing in the future. He asks for your forgiveness. You tell him he's forgiven.

Then he says, "Am I going to have to pay for the repairs?" And you say, "You betcha." He frowns. "But I thought you forgave me!"

And then he asks, "Can I have the keys to the other car, so I can get back out with my friends?" Fat chance on that, right? Again he says, "I thought you forgave me!"

Forgiving someone for how they have sinned against us doesn't mean that any and all consequences for their actions are erased. When we sin against God, do we still face consequences for our actions? Of course we do.

Nor does forgiveness mean trust is instantly reestablished. There is a formula for trust being restored. It's this:

$$T = \frac{CB}{t}$$

Trust = Consistent Behavior over time. Trust comes back into a relationship when we see that old behaviors that led to past sin are being removed, and new habits are being formed.

You can learn to trust your spouse again when they've shown a consistent pattern of new behavior. It will take time. How much time? As much as it takes. The amount of time it takes to rebuild trust correlates to the depth of the hurt.

Here's another important caveat. Forgiving your spouse for how he or she has sinned against you in the past does not mean that you enable the same kind of sin in the future. Enabling sin, or covering it up, will harm you both. Instead, you become an ally with your spouse in helping him or her break destructive patterns.

We've already seen what the Bible says in Galatians 6: "If anyone is caught in any transgression, you who are spiritual should restore him in a spirit of gentleness. Keep watch on yourself, lest you too be tempted. Bear one another's burdens, and so fulfill the law of Christ" (vv. 1–2).

These verses talk about a repeated pattern of sin, or what's sometimes called a besetting sin. It's a sin habit that is hard to break. That's what being "caught in a transgression" means. It's a picture of someone who is ensnared and can't get free.

While you are called to forgive the repeated offense, you are also called to be actively involved in seeking to restore the person who is trapped. Your job is to help them get free from their snare.

The passage makes it clear that if you're going to be an ally helping your spouse break free from a habitual sin, you need to be "spiritual." You need to have the right frame of mind. Be prayed up. Step into the battle with no motive other than to help your spouse be free from what both of you recognize as a sinful habitual pattern.

The passage also makes it clear that you can't do this without maintaining a spirit of gentleness. If you are harsh or bitter or angry, you're not in the right place spiritually to be trying to help someone else with his or her sin issues. You have issues of your own to work on! "Keep watch on yourself," we're told. The work can be discouraging. Frustrating. It will be easy for you to fall into sin patterns of your own. It will be easy for you to become self-righteous and critical, to lose sight of your own failings and shortcomings. To maintain a spirit of gentleness and to continue to be spiritually minded means that you have to stay humble.

It will be hard work. It will be easy to become weary. Pride and bitterness will be crouching at the door while you seek to be an ally to your spouse. You will need to depend mightily on God's grace. But this is what bearing one another's burdens is all about.

Again, you're not serving your spouse if you are covering up or enabling a sin pattern. You serve your spouse when you come alongside them and do what you can to help them be free from the ongoing sin pattern in their life. And you don't withhold grace and mercy and forgiveness until your spouse has the problem licked. You keep on forgiving while you simultaneously roll up your sleeves and say to your spouse, "I'm here for you and here to help you get free from this snare you're in."

No one is suggesting this whole process is easy or simple. It is an act of grace for us to absorb an offense and choose to forgive. It is a Spirit-empowered response to being sinned against.

"Forgiveness," author Dave Harvey says, "is not the stuff of an extraordinary saint. Forgiveness is at the heart of the Gospel and therefore is to be a defining characteristic of every believer."[2]

And author and counselor Lou Priolo doesn't mince words: "It's nothing but sheer wickedness for you not to forgive your offender for what he's done, in light of all that you've been forgiven (by Christ). When you compare the trivial offenses which you must forgive, with the enormous, eternal offenses you've committed against a holy God, the point is uncontestable."[3]

To forgive is more than a requirement though. It's an essential ingredient for a marriage to be what God intends for it to be.

Author's Note: I can't leave this subject of forgiveness without addressing the all-too-common issue of domestic violence and abuse that is present in so many marriages. I wouldn't want anyone reading these chapters to think that the biblical call to forgive someone means that God expects an abused spouse to continually put himself or herself in harm's way.

If abuse is present in your marriage, you need both spiritual and physical protection via church leaders and law enforcement authorities. Sadly, I've heard of too many cases where church leaders have not protected an abused spouse from an abuser.

For additional help on this subject, let me encourage you to get a copy of the book *Is It My Fault?* by Justin and Lindsey Holcomb (Moody Publishers, 2014). Take the necessary steps to protect yourself from abuse. He or she may try to use the biblical commands to forgive to manipulate you into silence. You are not loving an abuser when you continue to enable their sin against you.

PRACTICAL STEPS FOR REAL CHANGE

Are there offenses your spouse has committed against you where you are still holding onto anger, bitterness, hurt, resentment, or hatred? Are you harboring an unforgiving spirit, thinking that by doing so, you're somehow protecting yourself or getting justice for the wrong that was done to you?

Look at these passages that talk about how God deals with our sins:

> As far as the east is from the west, so far does he remove our transgressions from us. (Psalm 103:12)

In love you have delivered my life from the pit of destruction, for you have cast all my sins behind your back. (Isaiah 38:17b)

I, I am he who blots out your transgressions for my own sake, and I will not remember your sins. (Isaiah 43:25)

He will again have compassion on us; he will tread our iniquities underfoot. You will cast all our sins into the depths of the sea. (Micah 7:19)

How do these verses speak to the way we should respond to our spouse's sins against us?

Take ten minutes to pray your way through the verses below. Ask God to show you where you need to apply these passages in your marriage:

Be kind to one another, tenderhearted, forgiving one another, as God in Christ forgave you. (Ephesians 4:32)

Judge not, and you will not be judged; condemn not, and you will not be condemned; forgive, and you will be forgiven. (Luke 6:37)

Bearing with one another and, if one has a complaint against another, forgiving each other; as the Lord has forgiven you, so you also must forgive. (Colossians 3:13)

PART 4
RESTORING WHAT HAS BEEN BROKEN

Chapter 14

A NEW MARRIAGE WARDROBE

If you've heard the name John Gottman, you're probably also familiar with his famous "four horsemen of the marriage apocalypse." Gottman, a professor emeritus in psychology at the University of Washington, is well known for research he led in the 1970s and 1980s, in which his team observed the way spouses interacted with each other to see if they could find patterns common to marriages that ultimately ended in divorce.

He found four characteristics that repeatedly showed up. Those characteristics are what became known as the four horsemen of the marriage apocalypse: criticism, contempt, defensiveness, and stonewalling. Gottman found that when these four things regularly appeared as couples engaged in conflict, those couples were rarely able to make any progress toward oneness in their marriage.

Criticism. Contempt. Defensiveness. And stonewalling. I sat with a friend at lunch recently, talking about these four characteristics. He looked back at me and said, "We have all four in our marriage." And he was able to see how he was guilty of all of them in how he spoke to his wife.

He is not alone.

The danger these four horsemen present to a marriage is important enough that I should take just a minute to unpack how the Gottman Institute describes each one of the four horsemen.[1]

Criticism is when someone moves from complaining about a specific behavior to attacking another person's character. "You almost never get home when you say you will" addresses behavior. But when followed up with something like, "I can't believe anything you tell me! You're so irresponsible!" now they've moved to criticism.

Criticism opens the door to contempt. Contempt involves treating someone with disrespect, sarcasm, and ridicule. It communicates that the other person is worthless and despised. "Contempt," according to the Gottman researchers, "is fueled by long simmering negative thoughts about the partner . . . *Contempt is the single greatest predictor of divorce. It must be eliminated.*"[2]

The third horseman, defensiveness, is how most of us respond to criticism. We seek to justify, rationalize, excuse, or explain away our actions. We shift blame. We minimize. When our spouse brings up hurtful things we've said or ways we've been selfish, we tell them, "You're making way too big a deal about this." In doing so, we devalue what they're trying to tell us. We fail to take their concerns seriously. Defensiveness will only escalate the conflict. It's really a way of blaming our partner and refusing to accept responsibility for our role in the conflict.

Stonewalling is when we shut down, withdraw, and refuse to interact. We walk away. We won't engage. And because repairing what's broken in a relationship requires that both husband and wife be willing to address and own their part in the conflict, stonewalling is a path to nowhere. Nothing gets fixed by stonewalling.

Because of the danger criticism, contempt, defensiveness, and stonewalling pose, it's important to be able to recognize them. That's just the start, however; "To drive away destructive communication and conflict patterns, you must replace them with healthy, productive ones."[3]

Centuries before Dr. Gottman and his team identified the four horsemen of the marriage apocalypse and pointed to the need to replace bad patterns with productive ones, the Bible made the same observation.

In his letter to the Christians in the ancient city of Colossae, the apostle Paul identified more than four horsemen that can destroy a relationship. His list includes "sexual immorality, impurity, passion, evil desire, and covetousness, which is idolatry" (Colossians 3:5). These attitudes and behaviors, he said, have to be "put to death." Not managed. Not excused. What's on this list has to die.

He went on to tell his readers that they must also put away "anger, wrath, malice, slander, and obscene talk" as well as lying (Colossians 3:8–9).

The Bible's lists seem obvious, right? How can any marriage thrive if sexual immorality, evil desires, covetousness, anger, slander, cursing, and lying are part of the way we interact with our spouse?

The problem is, some of these attitudes or behaviors have become ingrained habits. And ridding your marriage of these noxious weeds is no simple feat. The Bible calls these things "what is earthly in you" (Colossians 3:5). In other words, when these habits become a regular part of your relationship, you're acting like a fallen sinful human being, not like a redeemed child of God. It takes a Holy Spirit-empowered commitment and persistent, diligent effort on your part to strip away what is in you that does not fit your identity as a follower of Jesus.

But as Dr. Gottman observed about the four horsemen of the marital apocalypse, getting rid of the destructive patterns in your relationship is just part of the process. You're going to have to begin the work of replacing bad habits, while you simultaneously cultivate new ways of interacting with your spouse.

Paul had a list for this too: "Put on then, as God's chosen ones, holy and beloved, compassionate hearts, kindness, humility, meekness, and patience, bearing with one another and, if one has a complaint against another, forgiving each other; as the Lord has forgiven you, so you also must forgive" (Colossians 3:12–13).

That's quite a list. A total character makeover, with a complete new wardrobe. There's a lot here for any of us to begin to cultivate.

The "put on" list begins by telling us that we are to have compassion for one another. Having compassion for another person means we come alongside someone who is suffering and suffer along with them. It means when someone is hurting, we hurt with them and for them.

Kindness is more than just being nice. To be kind means to make personal sacrifices that will help another person thrive. A kind person says, "My goal is your good."

Humility is having a proper perspective on our own worth or value—not thinking too highly of ourselves or too lowly of ourselves. From that foundation, as humble persons we will put the needs of others ahead of our own needs. "Do nothing from selfish ambition or conceit," the Bible says, "but in humility count others more significant than yourselves. Let each of you look not only to his own interests, but also to the interests of others" (Philippians 2:3–4). That's the mindset of someone who is humble.

Meekness requires the ability to govern passions and emotions. A meek person is not a weak person. A meek person has self-control, even in settings where tempers flare and anger is kindled. A meek person does not become the Incredible Hulk when he or she is angry.

Meekness goes hand in hand with patience. A patient person is someone who is able to bear up under hardship.

Older translations of the Bible use the term "long-suffering" as a synonym for patience. Patience is more than not losing your cool. It's maintaining your composure and your perspective and valuing the relationship more than your preferences or desires.[4]

To make progress toward oneness in a relationship, you have to be committed to stripping away the toxins that can easily destroy a marriage and replacing them with the antibodies that will keep your marriage healthy and strong. The good news is that when you make it a priority to put to death what is of the flesh and to cultivate that which is of the Spirit, you are aligning your life with God's will for you. It is his purpose for you to be "conformed to the image of his Son" (Romans 8:29). And to enable you to accomplish his purpose, he gives you the power you need through his Holy Spirit.

PRACTICAL STEPS FOR REAL CHANGE

Think about the four horsemen talked about in this chapter: criticism, contempt, defensiveness, and stonewalling. To what extent are any of these four characteristics present in your marriage? Would your spouse agree with your assessment?

Slowly and prayerfully review this list from Colossians 3 of things we need to "put to death." As you consider each behavior or attitude, ask yourself which of these is a sin pattern in your life that needs to be uprooted and exterminated. Which would your spouse identify?

- sexual immorality
- impurity
- passion
- evil desire
- covetousness
- anger
- wrath
- malice
- slander
- obscene talk
- lying

What specific steps can you take this week to begin to put the behaviors or attitudes you identified to death?

Now slowly and prayerfully review this list from Colossians 3 of spiritual attributes that ought to be pursued and cultivated. Again, ask yourself which one or two of these attributes need the most focused attention in your life? What would your spouse pick for you?

- compassion
- kindness
- humility
- meekness
- patience
- forbearance
- forgiveness
- love
- peacefulness
- thanksgiving

What specific steps can you take now to help you grow in the specific character qualities that you need to cultivate?

Pray and ask God for the empowering work of his Spirit as you begin putting on your new spiritual wardrobe.

Chapter 15

MARRIAGE BEST PRACTICES: EXTRAVAGANT LOVE

As we talked about in the previous chapter, John Gottman's research identified four habits or practices that show up in the interactions of couples who are on a path to isolation and divorce.

In this part of the book, I want us to think about four habits or practices that I believe regularly show up in strong, healthy marriages. It's hard to imagine any marriage falling into disrepair when these four best practices are present.

The first best practice is one we've already looked at, but it's worth revisiting for just a minute. In part 3 of this book, we talked about dealing with anger. About deciding whether to confront your spouse about an offense or to simply overlook it. About seeking forgiveness when you've sinned against your spouse. About granting forgiveness when you've been wronged. And about rebuilding trust when it has been broken.

At the heart of a couple's ability to resolve conflict should be *generous forgiveness*. As I've already said, your marriage will never be what God designed it to be without the essential oil of forgiveness and grace for one another. It's crucial for a strong, enduring marriage.

And so following what the Bible teaches about generous forgiveness in marriage is at the top of my list of best practices for marriage. It's a nonnegotiable. But there are three more best practices to consider. The second is *extravagant love*.

When most of us hear the term *extravagant*, we immediately think of money. And while extravagant love will be costly at some level, it's not money I have in mind. The kind of love I'm talking about here is a love that communicates to your spouse that he or she is treasured, highly valued, and deeply appreciated. It's a love that places your spouse's interests and needs above your own. That is extravagant love.

The *Merriam-Webster Dictionary* defines *extravagant* as "exceeding the limits of reason or necessity," "lacking in moderation, balance, and restraint," and "spending much more than necessary."

To be sure, the Bible calls us to be wise stewards of our financial resources. When it comes to money, thrift is a virtue. But when it comes to love, it's a different story. Think for a second about how you approach money and finances. On a scale of 1–5, where would you plot your financial temperament?

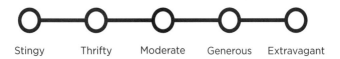

Stingy   Thrifty   Moderate   Generous   Extravagant

Most of us think that stinginess and extravagance are unhealthy extremes when it comes to money. We would probably aim for moderation, being thrifty when necessary and being generous when it's called for. We would avoid the extremes on either end of the scale.

But when it comes to expressing love for your spouse, the scale should shift. Unlike money, love is not a fixed asset you need to conserve. As a Christian, you have available to you an endless supply of love that you can draw from and shower on others. It is God's design and intent that you should be generous and even extravagant in how you demonstrate your love for your spouse.

Now take a minute to think about the way you show love to your spouse. On the 1–5 scale above, where do you see yourself? Where do you think your spouse sees you?

An essential feature of the extravagant love we're talking about is that it is, by God's design, exclusive. You don't express extravagant love with just anyone. In fact, it would be inappropriate to do so. Such love is something you reserve for your spouse. Part of what makes it extravagant is its exclusivity.

And extravagant love is a choice we make. It's not a feeling. It's something we decide to do, regardless of our circumstances and regardless of how our spouse responds. It is a decision of the will, not an emotional whim. We do it because it's what we promised we would do—love, honor, and cherish.

It's also a reflection of God's love for us. In 1 John 3, the Bible describes God's love for his children as a kind of love we've never seen before. We're told to pause and ponder the remarkable love God has demonstrated for us: "See [or Behold] what great love the Father has lavished on us" (1 John 3:1 NIV).

The English language doesn't really capture the intensity of what John is saying here. The word translated "see" or "behold" in this passage means to "take a good, hard, long look at" or "stare at and be amazed."

We're told in the Bible to think long and hard about the width and length and height and depth of God's love for us (Ephesians 3:18). When we gaze intently on the reality of God's remarkable love for us, what we're looking at is something completely new. In the original language, John is saying something like this: "Take a long hard look at this love from God. You are seeing a kind of love that is totally foreign to you. A kind of love that comes from somewhere you've never been. A kind of love that blows away all your categories for what love is."

It's extravagant love. And it's demonstrated for us in God's willingness to offer his beloved Son to pay the debt we owe for our sin. On the night before Jesus showed his love for us by going to the cross, he gave his disciples a new commandment: "love one another," he told them, "as I have loved you" (John 13:34).

Your love for one another in marriage should be a reflection of the lavish, extravagant kind of love God has exhibited for us. Jesus loved us lavishly. That's how you should love each other.

Your love for one another should be the kind of "greater love" Jesus talks about in John 15:13: "Greater love has no one than this, that someone lay down his life for his friends."

To lay down your life for someone would certainly qualify as a grand gesture. But day in, day out extravagant love in marriage is often made up of an ongoing stream of small, sacrificial acts of service like carrying the laundry to the laundry room or taking care of the dog when you'd rather veg out watching Sports Center. Marriages thrive when husbands and wives make a regular practice of finding simple ways to express their love for one another, when they are intentional about creatively expressing to each other "I care about you. I value you. You matter to me."

Cultivating the best practice of expressing extravagant love for your spouse may mean adding a prompt in your calendar as a reminder. Find a way to ask yourself a couple of times a week, *Have I expressed my love for my spouse this week? And was I extravagant or thrifty? How can I excel still more?*

As you set about expressing your extravagant love to your spouse, you need to make sure that you're communicating it in a way that is meaningful to them. A lot of couples get tripped up in their attempt to communicate their love for one another because they speak in a foreign language when trying to express it.

Let me explain what I mean.

In his best-selling book *The Five Love Languages*, Dr. Gary Chapman explains that each of us has a preferred love language. When Mary Ann and I read this book, it was a game changer for us. In the book, Dr. Chapman says that five common categories describe how we try to express our love for others:

1. quality time
2. acts of service
3. gifts
4. physical touch
5. words of encouragement

After many years of working with married couples, Dr. Chapman came to realize that each of us values these five ways of expressing love differently. For some people, quality time together is much more meaningful and affirming than a gift or physical touch. For others, words of encouragement are what matter most.

Most of us will instinctively express our love for our spouse using the categories that mean the most to us. But what if our spouse speaks a different love language?

Early in our marriage, I couldn't understand why my regular, generous words of affirmation and encouragement meant so little to Mary Ann. After reading Dr. Chapman's book, I realized that spending quality time with her and taking the initiative to perform acts of service were much more meaningful to her than all of my encouraging words.

I remember the night it dawned on me. We were with a group of other married couples, and the statement each of us was thinking about was this: "Share a time recently when your spouse did something that you found romantic."

When the question was posed to the group, I was in a bit of a panic. *What is Mary Ann going to come up with?* I wondered. I could think of things I'd done when we were dating that would qualify as romantic. But we'd been married now for a decade! What had I done recently?

When it came her time to speak, Mary Ann didn't hesitate. "The other night," she said, "while I was washing the dishes, and Bob was watching TV, he got up without me asking, turned off the TV, and came into the kitchen and starting drying the dishes. All on his own!"

I was stunned. Mary Ann saw drying dishes as romantic? As an expression of my love for her? That was news to me!

To demonstrate extravagant love in your marriage, you first have to know your spouse's love language then learn to speak it fluently.

Ultimately, extravagant love is a love that says, "I will sacrifice to show my love for you in a way that is meaningful for you. I will put your needs ahead of my own. I will serve you because I love you."

That's extravagant love. Is that present in your marriage? How often? What can you do this week to turn up the gain on that?

PRACTICAL STEPS FOR REAL CHANGE

As I said in this chapter, showing your spouse extravagant love is a decision, not a feeling. It's something you choose to do first and foremost because God is pleased when you choose to love each other.

List three ways you can demonstrate extravagant love for your spouse this week.

As you look at your list, are you sure that what you have in mind will communicate love to your spouse in his or her language? If not, find time this week to have a discussion about whether your assumptions about your spouse's love language are accurate and about how you can begin to more effectively express your love for one another.

Chapter 16

MARRIAGE BEST PRACTICES: ENTHUSIASTIC ENCOURAGEMENT

When I was a sophomore in high school, I was on the cross-country team. For that one season only. It happened by mistake—it's a long story.

I was not very good. I usually finished the race somewhere in the middle of the pack. But I learned a lesson in my one year of cross-country that I've never forgotten.

The course we ran for our home meets was in a local park. The path was a figure eight. We started the race by running a route that looped for a little more than a mile in one direction before coming back to the starting line. After we had run the first loop, we followed a different trail that took us out and back again. So the starting point, the midpoint, and the finish line of the race were all in the same spot.

We did not draw huge crowds for our cross-country meets. We had coaches, a few spectators, and a handful of cheerleaders who faithfully came out to urge us forward. When the gun went off to start the race, the small crowd cheered. And when they did, I found that my stride was brisk. But halfway around the first loop, when no one was watching me or cheering me on, my pace dragged. I began to ease up a bit. I wasn't going to win anyway. Why push myself?

As I completed the first loop and headed to the midpoint of the race, back where the coaches and cheerleaders were, I could hear some of the spectators spurring me on by name. "Go, Bob! You can do it." And guess what. I found myself working a little harder and picking up my pace as I heard them cheering for me. Suddenly, I had motivation and energy I hadn't had just a few hundred feet back.

The second loop followed the same pattern. I lagged in the middle. But as the finish line came into view, and as spectators cheered for me, my speed increased. For some reason, having people cheering gave me speed and strength I didn't know I had.

You've seen this at sporting events. Even professional athletes, people at the top of their game who are being paid handsomely to perform, will wave their arms as a signal to the fans to get louder. No matter who you are, there is something about having another person cheering you on that calls you up.

I love the way my friend Robyn McElvey describes it. Robyn was a high school cheerleader. "Our football team was pretty stinky," she says. "But even when they were way behind in the fourth quarter, with no way to win, we still cheered for them. That's what cheerleaders do."

Robyn likes to say that when a wife gets married she trades her wedding dress for a cheerleader uniform. Part of her job is to cheer her husband on. He needs her encouragement and her support. He picks up the pace when he hears his wife telling him, "You can do it. I believe in you."

It works both ways. Wives need their husbands to encourage and affirm and cheer for them as well. In healthy, thriving marriages, husbands and wives are cheerleaders for one another. Smart husbands and smart wives know that the Bible is right on target when it says, "Death and life are in the power of the tongue" (Proverbs 18:21). Spoken words can destroy or empower.

How do you and your spouse speak to each other? Do you build each other up? Or are your words critical and cutting? Think back to Dr. John Gottman's four horsemen of the marriage apocalypse—criticism, contempt, defensiveness, and stonewalling. It's the words you use with one another—and the words you fail to say—that expose these corrosive elements in marriage.

The Bible points us to a better way. In the book of James, our tongue is compared to a forest fire. In the same way that a simple spark can set acres ablaze, so a simple sentence can inflict great damage on a relationship. "No human being can tame the tongue," James says. "It is a restless evil, full of deadly poison. With it we bless our Lord and Father, and with it we curse people who are made in the likeness of God. From the same mouth come blessing and cursing. My brothers, these things ought not to be so" (3:8–10).

But there is an antidote to the deadly poison James talks about. It's found in Ephesians 4. There we're told we should "Let no corrupting talk come out of your mouths, but only such as is good for building up, as fits the occasion, that it may give grace to those who hear" (v. 29).

That verse provides the road map for how we should and shouldn't speak to one another in marriage. First, we're to eliminate *corrupting talk*. In the original language, the word translated "corrupting" is most often associated with food that is spoiling or rotting. Not only does the decay make the rotten food inedible; it spreads and destroys anything and everything it touches.

No doubt people have said things to you that have lodged in your soul and have had a putrefying effect on your self-confidence or your self-image. Maybe a careless or casual comment that another person made to you has haunted you for years. That's the power of corrupting talk. Once a destructive seed is planted in your soul, the bitter fruit grows for a long time. What sprouts from those seeds can be quite difficult to uproot.

The first step to becoming an enthusiastic encourager in your marriage is to guard your tongue. Eliminate any patterns of corrupting talk that may exist.

I grew up in a home where we showed affection for one another by teasing each other. A little good-natured verbal sparring was part of how we related to one another. My wife grew up in a different environment. In her home, instead of good-natured teasing, there was sarcasm that was harsh and hurtful. To her, then, my family's teasing came across entirely differently.

Out of love for Mary Ann, I had to learn how to adjust the way I spoke to her. What seemed like harmless banter to me was corrupting talk for her. I could have easily dismissed her feelings and concluded that she was overreacting or being hypersensitive. But the truth was, my words were hurtful, not helpful, so I needed to get rid of them.

Corrupting speech involves much more than sarcasm. Insults, profanity, lies or exaggeration, gossip, flattery, coarse jesting—these are just some ways in which our speech is dishonoring to God and can have a harmful effect on our marriage.

Psalm 34:13 is clear: "Keep your tongue from evil and your lips from speaking deceit." Eliminating corrupting talk in your marriage means you have to discipline yourself to think before you speak. You have to slow down, especially when you are stressed or angry. You have to weigh your words. You have to ask the question, will what I'm about to say tear down or build up my spouse?

You can help one another in this area if you're both humble and teachable. Cultivate the practice of asking one another a couple of times each week, "Have I said anything this week that has stuck with you that was hurtful or harmful?" If your spouse remembers something, don't become defensive. Apologize. Seek forgiveness. The goal is to become more aware of how things we say casually or carelessly can do real damage to our relationships.

Making it a priority to eliminate words that wound—corrupting talk—is how the journey toward being an enthusiastic encourager begins, but it doesn't end there. Just as we were told to put off sinful thoughts and practices and replace them with godly ones, here we're told that we should replace corrupting talk with words that are *good for building up*: words that give life, strength, and shelter to another person.

The word in the Bible that we translate "building up" or "edifying" is actually a construction word. I don't know if you've ever followed a building project from the beginning stages of raw land and a dream through to the ribbon cutting, but it's a fascinating process to watch. First, blueprints are created. Then the ground is prepared. A foundation is planned and poured. From there, the frame goes up, and the structure begins to take shape. It takes months of planning and labor for the building to emerge. But every step of the way, every person that is involved in the project, every nail that is pounded, every brick that is laid, every pipe that is fitted, and every piece of drywall that is hung—everything moves the project forward toward its ultimate goal.

As the spouse God has given your husband or wife, you are one of the means he uses to build them up. And you want your words to help them live out their identity as a new creation (2 Corinthians 5:17). With anything you say to your spouse, you should pause first and ask yourself, *Will what I'm about to say make him or her stronger? More stable? More durable?*

In addition to building your spouse up, your speech is supposed to *fit the occasion*. It's not just *what* you say that matters. *When* you say it, *how* you say it, *where* you say it—all of it is important. What time of day is best for this conversation? Should what I have to say be shared in private and not in front of others? If your spouse is focused on something else at the moment—like the last two minutes of a close game on TV—unless the house is on fire or there is some other emergency at hand, it's a good idea to push pause and hold off on the conversation.

Fitting the occasion is not only a question of time or place. You need to take your spouse's mental and emotional state into account. Show empathy: as you think about how and when to engage in a particular conversation, ask yourself about your spouse's current frame of mind. Through the years, my wife learned that first thing in the morning is not a good time to try to initiate a significant conversation with me. And I knew that right before bedtime was a bad time for her. We had to find ways to carve out the right moments for important conversations to happen. And honestly, there were times when it wasn't easy! But we found it was better to have the interaction at the right time for both of us than it was for us to try to rush things.

Finally, Ephesians 4:29 says that our words should always "give grace to those who hear." The best way to think about giving grace to someone is by asking if what we're about to say is going to be a gift or a lump of coal. Even then, even when we do our best to use carefully chosen words, we need to recognize that when we speak the truth in love (Ephesians 4:15) the truth can be hard to hear. Grace-filled speech can still be hurtful. The Bible calls them "the wounds of a friend" (Proverbs 27:6), but they're still wounds.

We don't have to scroll through social media long to find examples of speech that lacks grace, speech that tears down. But with grace, we are able to be agreeable, even when we disagree. We make room for the reality of imperfection. We take our shared frail humanity into account. We choose to overlook. We forgive. And our words reflect that perspective.

In Colossians 4 we see another aspect of grace-filled words. There we're told that our speech should always be "gracious, seasoned with salt" (v. 6). That's a curious expression until we think about the properties of salt. In the ancient world, it was used to preserve meat from decay and rot. It was put into a wound to prevent infection. It was also used as it is today, to make food more flavorful. Words that are full of grace keep rot out of a relationship and keep our wounds from becoming abscessed. Words seasoned with grace promote harmony and unity, not division and strife.

Your marriage should be like the "Home on the Range," "where seldom is heard a discouraging word and the skies are not cloudy all day."[1] The best marriages are filled with grace that pours forth in enthusiastic encouragement for one another. That's something worth cheering about.

PRACTICAL STEPS FOR REAL CHANGE

Specific encouragement is always better than general encouragement. "You're a great wife" is nice, but it's even nicer to hear, "One thing that makes you a great wife is _____."

With that in mind, come up with a list of ten specific things you can say to encourage your spouse. Use the prompts below to help get you started.

(A word of caution before you begin: be careful to avoid anything that could sound like correction or criticism. Don't be stingy with your words of encouragement. Avoid saying things like, "Occasionally, you _____" or "You do a decent job of _____" or "When you get around to _____, you do a decent job of it.")

1. "One of the ways you make my life better is by _____."
2. "Something I've always respected or admired about you is _____."

3. "You showed a lot of courage that time when
   _____."

4. "One thing you do really well—better than most—
   is _____."

5. "I'm grateful that I can depend on you to _____
   _____."

6. "A character quality of yours that I find particularly
   attractive is _____."

7. "I love the way you _____."

8. "One of the ways I've seen you grow recently is
   _____."

9. "I'm a better person when I'm with you because of
   your _____."

10. "The fruit of the Spirit (Galatians 5:22–23) that
    stands out in your life is _____
    _____. I saw it on display recently when _____
    _____."

Once you've completed your list, find a time when you can share it with your spouse. If you have a hard time saying something encouraging without wanting to add some kind of qualifier, you might need to practice first!

Then look for ways throughout the week to speak specific words of encouragement to your spouse.

Chapter 17

MARRIAGE BEST PRACTICES: COMMON CONVICTIONS

There's a classic roller-skating scene in the 1937 movie *Shall We Dance*, starring Ginger Rogers and Fred Astaire. The plot of the film has Fred, a ballet dancer, and Ginger, a show girl, dealing with rumors in the press that the two are secretly married.

"I don't know what to do," Ginger says.

"I don't either," says Astaire. Only he says it "eye-ther" and not "ee-ther."

Ginger rolls her eyes and corrects him: "The word is ee-ther."

That brings on a song where the two roller skate together and sing about their differences. "You like potato and I like potahto. You like tomato and I like tomahto." And their conclusion? "It's looks as if we two will never be one. . . . Let's call the whole thing off."[1]

The scene is on YouTube. It's worth watching.

Like Fred and Ginger, Mary Ann and I don't always see eye to eye. Most of the time, the things we don't agree on are trivial matters. Does the soup need more salt? Is the house too cold? Should we fill up the car at the gas station nearest our house or drive out to Costco to save a few bucks?

At the end of the day, whether the soup is too salty, the house is too hot, or we splurged on the convenience of a nearby gas station doesn't really matter. These are not hills to die on. And yet I've seen couples who have let trivial preferences divide them. For them, compromise even on inconsequential matters feels too much like surrender. And surrender feels disempowering. It feels risky.

I don't remember when it was, but there came a point in our marriage when it dawned on both of us that thinking differently about things and having differing opinions didn't mean one of us was right and the other was wrong. That idea became a mantra for us: *Different isn't necessarily wrong. Sometimes it's just different.* She wants chocolate peanut butter ice cream, and I want pecans, pralines, and cream? Fine! As long as something isn't dangerous or sinful, one view isn't right and the other wrong. *Vive la différence*!

Couples who never learn how to accept one another's preferences and idiosyncrasies are in for some hard sledding. When we make much out of differences that in the grand scheme of things don't really matter all that much, we are setting ourselves up for unnecessary discord in our marriage.

But some things are big things. There are some matters where husbands and wives need to be in alignment, and some are hills worth dying on. Three passages of Scripture can help us navigate issues of unity and difference.

First, Philippians 2, in which the apostle Paul writes about the importance of like-mindedness among believers. Think about how these first few verses apply to marriage. "So if there is any encouragement in Christ, any comfort from love, any participation in the Spirit, any affection and sympathy, complete my joy by being of the same mind, having the same love, being in full accord and of one mind. Do nothing from selfish ambition or conceit, but in humility count others more significant than yourselves. Let each of you look not only to his own interests, but also to the interests of others" (vv. 1–4).

The heart of the passage is a call to oneness—"being of the same mind, having the same love, being in full accord and of one mind." This is not a call for uniformity but for unity. The alignment of heart and mind that Paul is calling for here springs from verse 1—from our common experience of being in Christ. One translation of the passage talks about our unity being anchored in being "intent on one purpose" (Philippians 2:2 NASB). Pastor Kent Hughes says, "The unity Paul wants is not a vacuous togetherness but a oneness fraught with dynamic purpose."[2]

If all you're doing in your marriage is minimizing conflict with a "go along to get along" mindset, that's not unity. You're smart enough to realize that your unity as a couple should not be threatened by how one of you pronounces potato and tomato. But what Philippians 2 is saying is that your one-mindedness should be centered in your common experience of being in Christ and your common commitment to living out his purposes for your lives.

Having this common experience and commitment means that as a couple you should share the priorities God has ordained for all of us in his word. That's the kind of one-mindedness to which this passage is calling us. When the two of you aren't in agreement, you should be asking yourselves, What does God want for us in this case? His word, not your opinions or preferences, should be the fulcrum for your unity.

The passage goes on to say that this kind of God-centered unity is going to require major doses of humility. In speaking to couples over the years, I've often remarked that if a couple can live out in their marriage what we're called to in Philippians 2:3–4, most marital strife will be ended. When you chase away selfishness, count your spouse as more important than yourself, and look out for their interests as passionately as you look out for your own interests, your marriage will experience God's blessing and favor.

The bottom line of this passage is that your shared convictions as a couple should originate from your common faith in Christ and your common commitment to his purposes for your lives. When you're trying to get your spouse to line up with your preferences or what you think makes sense, you're headed into the swamp. But when both of you make God's Word and his priorities the centerpiece of your relationship, you're on the right track.

Our second passage makes it clear that we should allow plenty of room in our relationship for disagreements and differing opinions on disputed matters that aren't central to the faith. That's the main idea in Romans 14.

The chapter begins with a warning against quarreling or passing judgment when it comes to opinion or disputable matters. Eugene Peterson, in his paraphrase of the verse, says that the Bible is telling us not to "jump all over [people] every time they do or say something you don't agree with" (Romans 14:1 MSG).

The specific issues addressed in Romans 14 are diets and days. Some people in Paul's day refused to eat meat that had been offered to pagan idols. Others figured meat is meat. Additionally, there was a division between Christians who continued to observe the Jewish feasts and festivals and those who didn't. Paul essentially said to both groups "quit quarreling about it. And don't despise your brothers and sisters who think differently than you do."

If Philippians 2 is a call to gospel-focused unity in our marriage, Romans 14 is a call to gospel-infused diversity. Your love for your spouse should be stronger than your convictions about secondary matters where you disagree.

This doesn't mean that secondary matters are unimportant or insignificant. In your marriage, you'll face lots of challenges that will require biblically informed wisdom. Should you move to another city to pursue a career? What's the right choice when it comes to where your children go to school? How do you make wise financial decisions about things like saving, spending, or giving? Ultimately, you will need to apply biblical principles as you face these decisions. You should seek godly counsel from others. And you should spend time in prayer, asking God to direct your steps.

There will undoubtedly be times in your marriage when, after an extended season of dialogue, study, and prayer, you will still see things differently. In these situations, God lays the responsibility for the ultimate decision at the feet of the husband and calls on wives to respect and honor the decision the husband makes. This entire process should be wrapped in your love for each other and your commitment to unity as a couple.

This is where a third passage of Scripture can help us know how to walk together as we wrestle with our differences. In Ephesians 4, after spending three chapters explaining all that Jesus has done for us to reconcile us to God and to one another, Paul lays out this charge: "I . . . urge you to walk in a manner worthy of the calling to which you have been called, with all humility and gentleness, with patience, bearing with one another in love, eager to maintain the unity of the Spirit in the bond of peace" (vv. 1–3).

If you have children, I imagine you've taught them the right way to respond to someone who gives them a gift. We had to remind our children who were delighted (and distracted) by the gift they had just received to pause and say thank you.

The Bible tells us that the right way for us to express our thanks to God for the gift of his Son is to relate to others with humility, gentleness, patience, and forbearance. For us to claim that we are children of God and then to be annoyed, impatient, and arrogant with others is to dishonor the God who sent his Son to redeem us and make us into new people.

Along with calling us to humility, gentleness, patience, and forbearance, the passage tells us we should be "eager to maintain the unity of the Spirit in the bond of peace." When we stop to think about all God has done for us, unity in our marriage is something we should be eager to maintain. It's one of the ways we thank God for his grace in our lives.

These three passages can be summed up in an often-repeated statement that has been attributed to St. Augustine and others through the years: "In essentials, unity. In non-essentials, liberty. In all things, charity (love)."

Marriages that thrive have figured out what the essentials are. They leave room in their relationship for differences and preferences. In fact, they've learned how to celebrate their differences. They've come to realize that another viewpoint can be an asset. They've reached out to others for help and guidance when they reached an impasse. And keeping in mind the price Jesus paid to reconcile us to God and to each other, they have prioritized unity and peace in their relationship, with their love for each other at the center of everything.

The best practice of cultivating common convictions is key to such harmony. Together with the three other best practices—generous forgiveness, extravagant love, and enthusiastic encouragement—couples have the essential elements that form a stable foundation for any marriage. And God has given us his Word and his Spirit to empower us to live out these practices in our marriage.

There's only one problem. No matter how hard you try, you're going to fall short. Mess up. You're going to say things you wish you hadn't said. You'll do things you shouldn't have done. And you'll neglect matters that turn out to be more significant than you realized they'd be. Along the way, you'll wound each other.

This brings us back to grace. God pours out his grace on us when we blow it. And we in turn pour out grace when our spouse falls short. We forgive one another. We love each other. We encourage each other. And we recommit to bringing our lives and our marriage into alignment with God's design and purposes for us.

PRACTICAL STEPS FOR REAL CHANGE

Would you say you and your spouse are united on essential issues? If not, what essential issues need to be addressed? How can you get help addressing them?

Think about an issue in your marriage that has been a source of conflict, an area where you and your spouse don't agree. Ask yourself the following questions:

1. Is our disagreement over something that is clearly and explicitly addressed in Scripture?

   If so, is there a pastor or godly mentor you can enlist to help you think about what the Bible says on the issue and how to address it with your spouse?

2. Is our disagreement a matter of preference?

   If so, what happens if you defer to your spouse? What happens if your spouse defers to you? How can you work together to resolve this issue? If this is something that must be decided (you can't just agree to disagree), and if you have prayed and have tried and been unable to resolve this matter yourselves, you might want to consider bringing in a pastor or godly mentor to help you.

CONCLUSION

REAL CHANGE
REQUIRES REAL CHANGE

Yes. You read that right. Real change (in your marriage) requires real change (in you). You may be able to put a patch on something to get it working temporarily. But if you want to do more than just limp along, things must change.

And by *things*, I mean *you*.

Jesus made at least three promises to you when you decided to follow him. First, he promised to forgive your sins. Second, he promised to give you new life. And third, he promised you a hope and a future.

Forgiveness. Transformation. Hope. For all who will believe in him and follow him. That's the promise of the gospel. That's good news.

Most people I've met who profess faith in Jesus understand their need for forgiveness. The promise that "there is therefore now no condemnation for those who are in Christ Jesus" (Romans 8:1) is a glorious promise. Our guilt and shame are removed from us when we trust in Christ. Who wouldn't want the Judge of the universe to declare their crime has been covered and they are free to go?

And most churchgoing people I know have a hope for the future. They believe in life after death, and they find comfort in the promise Jesus made to his followers—that he would go and prepare a place for them where they will be with him forever (John 14:1–3).

It's the promise of transformation that I've seen people get stuck on. Forgiven sins? Yes, please. Heaven? Again, yes. But change? Me? I'm not so sure about that.

The reason for the reluctance when it comes to change is that most of us think we don't need to change. Our main problems, as we see it, are outside of us, not inside of us. We think it's the people around us who need to change. Or we think our circumstances are our biggest problem. When it comes right down to it, when we look at the problems and challenges we're facing, we're not convinced that the issue is us.

I know a lot of people who claim to be Christians who believe their sins have been forgiven and who expect they will be in heaven one day but who don't see a need for any change in their lives. But that's not how salvation works. Forgiveness and hope are tied to the realization that our life needs to be transformed and our willingness to surrender to Jesus's purposes for us. We can't say to God, "I'd like the salvation special, but hold the life change, please."

If you're serious about wanting to see a change in your marriage, maybe the most important step forward is for you to take a good, long, honest, hard look at your spiritual condition. Author and speaker Don Whitney has developed a series of questions that can help you diagnose your level of spiritual health. Read through the questions below, and take the time to honestly grapple with them:

- Do you thirst for God?
- Are you governed increasingly by God's Word?
- Are you more loving?
- Are you more sensitive to God's presence?
- Do you have a growing concern for the spiritual and temporal needs of others?
- Do you delight in the bride of Christ [the local church]?
- Are the spiritual disciplines [such as _____] increasingly important to you?

- Do you still grieve over sin?
- Are you a quick forgiver?
- Do you yearn for heaven and to be with Jesus?[1]

I don't know you. But most of the churches I've visited or spoken at through the years are filled with sincere, polite men and women who profess faith in Jesus but who are only nominally interested in spiritual things. They don't read their Bibles much. Prayer is an afterthought. They go for days without ever thinking about God and his purposes for them or for our world. They quickly excuse their sin.

A pastor friend I know has a name for these people. He calls them "unsaved Christians."[2]

The most important factor in determining the success of your marriage is whether or not you have a vibrant, vital, growing, authentic relationship with Jesus, individually and as a couple. You may have prayed a prayer at some point, asking Jesus into your life. You may have walked down an aisle, joined a church, or thrown a stick in a fire at youth camp. My question for you today is whether any of those moments in your past have reshaped your life and your priorities.

Recently a doctor prescribed me a round of antibiotics for a bacterial infection I had contracted. I faithfully took my meds four times a day every day for fourteen days. A few weeks later, I went back to the doctor for a checkup. He ran a few tests and called me the next day with the results. The infection was still in my system. The antibiotics had failed to do the job.

A lot of people I know think that as long as they've prayed a prayer once (or twice or a dozen times), they are all squared away spiritually. But if there's no life change taking place, they must ask themselves a hard question. For what exactly were they praying? Did they see the need for personal transformation when they prayed? Were they signing up to die to self, take up the cross, and follow Jesus wherever he would lead (Matthew 16:24)?

At the beginning of this book, I pointed you to these verses from Psalm 139. This is a good time for you to revisit them.

Search me, O God, and know my heart!
   Try me and know my thoughts!
And see if there be any grievous way in me,
   and lead me in the way everlasting! (vv. 23–24)

It's not my goal here to rattle the faith of any genuine child of God. The fact that you are experiencing challenges or disappointment in your marriage doesn't mean you're not a child of God. If you know and love Jesus, if he is the center of your life, and if you long for his kingdom to come and his will to be done on earth as it is in heaven, you can rest in the knowledge that he has promised to never leave you or forsake you. You belong to him.

But I do want to confront the complacency I see in the lives of many professing Christians today. Are you one of them? If so, my prayer is that this book will be a turning point not just in your marriage but in your life. My hope is that this would be a moment of fresh surrender for you— that you would confess your sin and your need for Jesus to forgive you for your complacency.

I told you at the beginning of this book that I have hope for your marriage, no matter where you are right now. That hope is founded in the promise of God to continue the good work he has begun in you (Philippians 1:6). As you continue to seek him, follow him, abide in him, and bring your burdens to him, he will continue to mold and shape you more and more into the image of his Son (Romans 8:29; 2 Corinthians 3:18). He is the God who turns "mourning into dancing" (Psalm 30:11).

May this be the first step toward a glorious new chapter in your marriage.

ACKNOWLEDGMENTS

You've no doubt heard about blind squirrels and acorns. Between 1992 and 2021, I had the distinct honor of serving as the cohost of *FamilyLife Today*®, a nationally syndicated radio program. Our objective was to provide listeners with practical, biblical help and hope for their marriage and their family. In that capacity, I had the unique opportunity to have long, deep conversations with hundreds of pastors, authors, theologians, scholars, and everyday husbands and wives about God's plan for marriage. The insights you find in this book are acorns that were shared with this blind squirrel!

In addition, I spent more than a quarter century speaking at Weekend to Remember marriage getaways across the country. Anyone who has attended one of those weekend events will hear echoes as they read these pages.

I want to thank the team at New Growth Press for the significant part they have played in shaping this book. I first met Mark and Karen Teears when New Growth Press was a dream. With hundreds of books published over the past fifteen-plus years, their vision has emerged as a great gift for the body of Christ. Special thanks to Marty Machowski, Barbara Juliani, Ruth Castle, and especially Susan Pitt-Davis, whose editorial input was invaluable.

Since 2008, I have had the joy of serving as a pastor to the faithful, hungry-hearted people who make up our congregation at Redeemer Community Church in Little Rock. I know many pastors who have faced hardships and challenges in ministry. Our church family has made my labor sweet.

Finally, my wife, Mary Ann, has been my ally, my confidant, my cheerleader, my coach, my best friend, and the great love of my life since we both said "I do" in 1979. What I know about commitment, sacrifice, and love I've learned from her.

Soli Deo Gloria!

ENDNOTES

Introduction

1. Names have been changed throughout the book to ensure privacy.

Chapter 2

1. Username Loloopy, "Microphone Holder (not provided)," Amazon customer review (October 15, 2018), https://www. amazon.com/product-reviews/B019NY2PKG/ref=acr_dp_ hist_1?ie=UTF8&filterByStar=one_star&reviewerType=all_ reviews#reviews-filter-bar.

Chapter 6

1. "About Child Trauma," National Child Traumatic Stress Network, https://www.nctsn.org/what-is-child-trauma/about-child-trauma.

Chapter 7

1. Wendy D. Manning and Bart Stykes, "Twenty-five Years of Change in Cohabitation in the U.S., 1987–2013" (FP-15-01), National Center for Family and Marriage Research, 2015, https:// www.bgsu.edu/content/dam/BGSU/college-of-arts-and-sciences/ NCFMR/documents/FP/FP-15-01-twenty-five-yrs-cohab-us.pdf.

2. Charitie Lees Bancroft, "Before the Throne of God Above," public domain.

Chapter 9

1. For help dealing with hurts from the past, see Brad Hambrick's book *Angry with God* (Greensboro, NC: New Growth Press, 2022).

2. Bob Bennett, "Lord of the Past," track 15 on *Lord of the Past: A Compilation*, Urgent Record, 2005, used with permission.

Chapter 12

1. Ruth Bell Graham and Gigi Graham Tchividjian, *A Quiet Knowing* (Nashville, TN: Thomas Nelson, 2001), 42.

2. *Fireproof*, movie directed by Alex Kendrick, produced by Alex and Stephen Kendrick and David Nixon (United States: Sherwood Pictures, 2008).

Chapter 13

1. Adapted from Ken Sande, *The Peacemaker: A Biblical Guide to Resolving Personal Conflict*, 3rd ed. (Grand Rapids, MI: Baker Books, 2004), 209; Relational Wisdom 360, https://rw360.org/biblical-forgiveness/.

2. Dave Harvey, *When Sinners Say "I Do"* (Wapwallopen, PA: Shepherd Press, 2007), 110.

3. Lou Priolo, *The Complete Husband* (Calvary Press, 1999), 111.

Chapter 14

1. You can read more about Gottman's work at Ellie Lisitsa, "The Four Horsemen: Criticism, Contempt, Defensiveness, and Stonewalling," https://www.gottman.com/blog/the-four-horsemen-recognizing-criticism-contempt-defensiveness-and-stonewalling/.

2. Lisitsa, "The Four Horsemen," emphasis in original.

3. Lisitsa, "The Four Horsemen."

4. For an extended look at what kindness, humility, and patience in marriage should look like, see chapters 2–4 of my book *Love Like You Mean It* (Nashville, TN: B&H Publishing, 2020).

Chapter 16

1. "Home on the Range," words based on the poem "My Home in the West" (1876), music by Daniel E. Kelley, public domain, https://www.loc.gov/item/ihas.200196571/.

Chapter 17

1. *Shall We Dance*, movie directed by Mark Sandrich, produced by Pandro S. Berman (United States: RKO Pictures, 1937).

2. R. Kent Hughes, *Philippians: The Fellowship of the Gospel* (Wheaton, IL: Crossway Books, 2007), 76.

Conclusion

1. Donald S. Whitney, *Ten Questions to Diagnose Your Spiritual Health* (Colorado Springs, CO: NavPress, 2001).

2. See Dean Inserra's book *The Unsaved Christian: Reaching Cultural Christianity with the Gospel* (Chicago: Moody Press, 2019).